LISBON

TOMAS TRANÆUS

EYEWITNESS TRAVEL

Left **Castelo de São Jorge** Centre **Archeological finds, Sé Catedral** Right **Praia da Bela Vista**

LONDON, NEW YORK,
MELBOURNE, MUNICH AND DELHI
www.dk.com

Produced by Coppermill Books
55 Salop Road London E17 7HS

Reproduced by Colourscan, Singapore
Printed and bound in China by Leo Paper
Products Ltd

First published in Great Britain in 2007
by Dorling Kindersley Limited
80 Strand, London WC2R 0RL
A Penguin Company

11 12 13 14 10 9 8 7 6 5 4 3 2

**Copyright 2007, 2011
© Dorling Kindersley Limited, London**

Reprinted with revisions 2009, 2011

All rights reserved. No part of this
publication may be reproduced, stored in a
retrieval system, or transmitted in any form
or by any means, electronic, mechanical,
photocopying, recording or otherwise,
without the prior written permission of the
copyright owner.

A CIP catalogue record is available from the
British Library.

ISBN 978 1 40536 086 9

Within each Top 10 list in this book, no
hierarchy of quality or popularity is implied.
All 10 are, in the editor's opinion, of roughly
equal merit.

MIX
Paper from
responsible sources
FSC
www.fsc.org   FSC™ C018179

Contents

Lisbon's Top 10

Castelo de São Jorge   8

Mosteiro dos Jerónimos   10

Sé Catedral   12

Museu Nacional
de Arte Antiga   14

Parque das Nações   16

Torre de Belém   18

Museu Nacional
do Azulejo   20

Palácio de Queluz   22

Museu Calouste
Gulbenkian   24

Sintra   26

The information in this DK Eyewitness Top 10 Travel Guide is checked regularly.
Every effort has been made to ensure that this book is as up-to-date as possible at the time of
going to press. Some details, however, such as telephone numbers, opening hours, prices,
gallery hanging arrangements and travel information are liable to change. The publishers cannot
accept responsibility for any consequences arising from the use of this book, nor for any
material on third party websites, and cannot guarantee that any website address in this book
will be a suitable source of travel information. We value the views and suggestions of our
readers very highly. Please write to: Publisher, DK Eyewitness Travel Guides,
Dorling Kindersley, 80 Strand, London WC2R 0RL, Great Britain or email: travelguides@dk.com.

Cover: Front – DK IMAGES: Linda Whitwam bl. PHOTOLIBRARY: photononstop/Tibor Bognor main. Spine – DK
IMAGES: Linda Whitwam b. Back – DK IMAGES: Linda Whitwam tc, tl; Peter Wilson tr.

Left **Parque das Nações** Centre **Art Nouveau tiles, Rua dos Sapateiros** Right **Rua Augusta**

Moments in History	30	
Churches and Monasteries	32	
Museums and Galleries	34	
City Views	36	
African Lisbon	38	
Shopping Districts	40	
Bars and Nightclubs	42	
Restaurants	44	
Culinary Highlights	46	
Beaches	48	
Activities for Children	50	
Excursions	52	

Around Town

Alfama, Castelo & the East	56
Baixa to Restauradores	62
Chiado & Bairro Alto	70
West Lisbon	80
Avenida & North Lisbon	90
Lisbon Coast	98

Streetsmart

Practical Information	106
Places to Stay	112
General Index	118
Acknowledgements	125
Phrase Book	126
Selected Street Index	128

Left **Torre de Belém** Right **Ponte 25 de Abril**

LISBON'S TOP10

Lisbon Highlights
6–7

Castelo de São Jorge
8–9

Mosteiro dos Jerónimos
10–11

Sé Catedral
12–13

Museu Nacional
de Arte Antiga
14–15

Parque das Nações
16–17

Torre de Belém
18–19

Museu Nacional
do Azulejo
20–21

Palácio de Queluz
22–23

Museu Calouste
Gulbenkian
24–25

Sintra
26–27

Top 10 of Everything
30–53

LISBON'S TOP 10

Lisbon Highlights

These days, fewer visitors approach Lisbon from the sea than once used to, but the wide turn many airliners make over the beach at Caparica – before crossing the river above the red suspension bridge and sweeping over the city's roofs to the airport – is a pretty good introduction too. Lisbon is a city of immediate charms, and of a deeper beauty that must be sought out. The light loves it, painting it in warm pink hues and bright blues. It is an old place, steeped in history, but not closed in on itself as it once was. Lisbon's youthful, modern side includes a nightlife which is among Europe's liveliest, latest and most diverse.

1 Castelo de São Jorge
Crowning the hill where Lisbon's original settlers lived, the city's medieval castle is a successful and evocative reconstruction. Best of all are the views from the esplanade *(see pp8–9)*.

2 Mosteiro dos Jerónimos
The Manueline is Portugal's own architectural style. Its beginnings, and some of its greatest expressions, can be seen in the glorious national monument that is the Jerónimos Monastery *(see pp10–11)*.

3 Sé Catedral
Lisbon's cathedral was built for the city's first bishop in the middle of the 12th century, just after the Christian reconquest. It is a fortress-like structure whose stone glows amber as the sun sets *(see pp12–13)*.

4 Museu Nacional de Arte Antiga
Housed in a grand 17th-century palace, Portugal's national gallery displays art that places Portugal in a historical context – as well as other treasures *(see pp14–15)*.

Preceding pages **Elevador da Bica**

Parque das Nações
Flanked by the Vasco da Gama Bridge, the site of Lisbon's sea-themed Expo 98 has been transformed into a dynamic leisure, business and residential area (see pp16–17).

Torre de Belém
The boot-shaped defensive tower at Belém is one of Lisbon's emblems, but it is also one of the most perfect examples of the Manueline style, with proportions that please, rather than inspire awe (see pp18–19).

Museu Nacional do Azulejo
This beautiful museum displays and explains the essential Portuguese decorative element – the tile. It also has some of the city's most stunning convent and church interiors (see pp20–21).

Palácio de Queluz
A Rococo feast, ripe with culture and aspiration, this summer palace just outside Lisbon was for a brief period the royal family's permanent residence. It still exudes an air of fussily ordered pleasure (see pp22–3).

Museu Calouste Gulbenkian
A museum of the highest international calibre, the Gulbenkian is a small, coolly pleasant universe of art history, where visitors can drift around oblivious of any other (see pp24–5).

Sintra
Sintra is a powerful magnet for most visitors to Lisbon, but it is wise to do as Lord Byron did, and absorb the city first before moving on to Sintra – the better to appreciate the contrast (see pp26–7).

🔟 Castelo de São Jorge

This hilltop castle is traditionally regarded as the site of Lisbon's founding settlement. Recent archeological finds dated to the 6th century BC support this theory, although the oldest castle remains are from the Moorish era. Portugal's first king, Afonso Henriques, captured the Moorish citadel in 1147 and his successors added the Alcáçovas palace, which remained the royal residence until 1511. Following centuries of neglect, the castle was imaginatively restored in 1938, providing Lisbon with one of its most attractive viewpoints.

Figure of St George

⏱ The west-facing esplanade is at its best in the late afternoon, with a low sun painting everything in warm hues. Early mornings here are shady, and can be chilly.

🍴 The outdoor bars at Chapitô or Bar das Imagens *(see p60 for both)* are good places to digest a visit to the castle.

- Porta de São Jorge, Rua do Chão da Feira
- Map G4
- 218 800 620
- Open 9am–9pm (6pm Nov–Feb) daily
- Adm €7 (concessions and family groups €3.50; under-10s free)
- Torre de Ulisses camera obscura open 10am–5pm daily (depending on visibility); castle museum open 9am–9pm (8pm Nov–Feb)

Top 10 Features

1. Porta de São Jorge
2. Esplanade
3. Statue of Afonso Henriques
4. Castle Museum
5. Casa do Leão
6. Inner Battlements
7. Torre de Ulisses
8. Torre de São Lourenço
9. Gardens
10. Santa Cruz Neighbourhood

1 Porta de São Jorge
This grand gate gives onto the final steep climb up to the castle grounds. In a wall niche to the left is a figure of St George *(above left)*. His local connection may derive from English troops' role in the conquest of Moorish Lisbon.

2 Esplanade
The esplanade on top of the outer fortifications is one of the main rewards of a climb up to the castle. Dotted with archeological remains and shaded by pines, it follows the castle's western perimeter, offering views of the river and the lower city *(below)*.

3 Statue of Afonso Henriques
This bronze statue of Portugal's first king was added to the esplanade in 1947. It is a copy of a romantic 1887 work by Soares dos Reis (the original is in Guimarães).

4 Castle Museum
On the site of the historic Alcáçovas palace, this museum contains a collection of artifacts excavated from the hilltop, such as Iron-Age cooking pots and 15th-century tiles.

Casa do Leão

5 This restaurant, in one of Lisbon's most exclusive locations, serves classic Portuguese and international food. The interior was part of the 13th-century Alcáçovas palace, but sit outside if you can; the views are superb.

Inner Battlements

6 The reconstruction of the inner castle is one of the great achievements of the 1938 restoration. With ten towers and a dividing inner wall, the restored castle matches, as far as possible, the original's layout and size.

Torre de Ulisses

7 In one of the inner battlement towers, a camera obscura attached to a periscope projects images of the city. The castle has a history of distant gazing: Lisbon's first observatory was set up there in 1779.

Torre de São Lourenço

8 Connected to the castle by a long series of steps *(right)*, this tower once formed part of the outer fortifications. Today, it offers another angle from which to view the castle.

Gardens

9 Don't miss the peacocks in the shady castle gardens – and look out for the excavations of a Moorish village.

Santa Cruz Neighbourhood

10 The tiny and partially restored neighbourhood of Santa Cruz do Castelo (within the old citadel) is one of the most picturesque parts of Lisbon *(left)*. It is home to ageing residents as well as younger investors and luxury hotels.

Mythical martyr

The myth of Martim Moniz, a soldier who is said to have given his life as a doorstopper in 1147, allowing Afonso Henriques and his crusaders to enter the castle, has a durable grip on the Lisboetan imagination. The gate where his unverified deed took place bears his name, as does a central Lisbon square below the castle.

Before it was restored, the Castle was a jumble of army and government buildings.

Mosteiro dos Jerónimos

Few of Lisbon's monuments are overly grand – and while this historic monastery is imposing, its proportions remain approachable. Built from the beginning of the 16th century by Diogo de Boytac and finally by Jerónimo de Ruão, Jerónimos is a celebration of Portugal's territorial expansion and an expression of a uniquely national style. It's also a monument to Portuguese identity, housing tombs of men who helped make the country great, including navigator Vasco da Gama, Dom Sebastião and poet Luís de Camões.

Manueline cloister

⚡ This is one of the most visited sites in Lisbon. Think twice before going at weekends, on mid-mornings or on mid-afternoons (the latter two are favoured by tour groups). Hit it at lunchtime, or just before it closes, when the stone turns honey-coloured.

🍷 One of the most serene places for a drink in Belém is the terrace café at the CCB (see p34), overlooking the river from a minimalist garden.

• Praça do Império
• Map B6
• 213 620 034
• Open 10am–6pm (5pm Oct–Apr) Tue–Sun; closed 25 Dec, 1 Jan, 1 May, Easter Sun
• Adm €7 (concessions €3.50; under-14s free; free before 2pm on Sun & public holidays)
• www.igespar.pt

Top 10 Features

1. South Portal
2. West Portal
3. Nave
4. Cloister
5. Refectory
6. Tombs of Vasco da Gama and Luís de Camões
7. Tombs of Dom Sebastião and Cardinal D. Henrique
8. Main Chapel
9. Chapterhouse
10. Extension

South Portal
Restraint might not be the word for this towering sculpture of an entrance *(above)*, but look closely and you'll see that none of its parts is overpoweringly large. The figures include Henry the Navigator.

West Portal
The mouldings and surrounds of this portal (used today as the main entrance) by French sculptor Nicolau Chanterène show the Manueline love of fantastical Renaissance decoration.

Nave
Many visitors find the well-lit nave *(above)* the most striking feature of Jerónimos, with its soaring pillars supporting a beautiful fan-vaulted ceiling.

Cloister
Begun by Diogo de Boytac and finished by João de Castilho and Diogo de Torralva, the cloister is a lesson in Manueline tracery and lavish ornament *(left)*.

The tomb of Dom Sebastião is empty, as the young king's body was never found after the battle of Alcácer-Quivir.

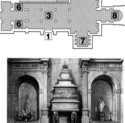

Refectory
The long, narrow refectory features fabulous vaulting and rope-like Manueline mouldings. The panel on the north wall depicts the biblical story of the feeding of the 5,000.

Tombs of Vasco da Gama and Luís de Camões
In the Lower Choir – facing the aisles under the gallery – are the tombs of Vasco da Gama *(below)* and Luís de Camões, transferred here in 1940.

Chapterhouse
Completed only in the 19th century, the attractive chapterhouse was never used as such. It houses the tomb of Alexandre Herculano, a celebrated 19th-century historian who also served as the first mayor of Belém.

Tombs of Dom Sebastião and Cardinal D. Henrique
As you pass under the stellar vault of the crossing, look to each side to see the grand tombs of Cardinal D. Henrique and Dom Sebastião *(above)*.

Main Chapel
The current main chapel, dating from 1572, has a gridlike Mannerist layout. Look here for the tombs of Dom Manuel I and his wife Dona Maria (on the left) and Dom João III and his wife Dona Catarina (on the right).

Extension
Major restoration and extension works in the 19th century saw the addition of the long, Neo-Manueline west wing *(below)*, which now houses the Museu de Arqueologia and part of the Museu da Marinha *(see p84)*. Another addition was the distinctive domed belltower (the previous roof was pointed).

Stone surprises
Spend some time studying the carvings on the pillars in the nave, and you may come across exotic plants and animals along with exquisite human faces and a few mythical figures. What better way to remind posterity that all this beauty was hewn by human hands, belonging to individuals and masons who would occasionally get bored, when carving.

For more examples of the Manueline style See p33

11

🔟 Sé Catedral

Lisbon's cathedral was built shortly after Dom Afonso Henriques had taken Lisbon from the Moors in 1147, and stands on on the site once occupied by the city's main mosque. The crenellated Romanesque building we see today is a restoration and reconstruction, because the cathedral suffered damage from earthquakes and was rebuilt in various architectural fashions. The Sé is also an important archeological site, with new finds made regularly beneath the cloister – originally excavated to reinforce the building's foundations.

Rose window

🔘 The Sé is a very dark church, and enlightenment seems a distant prospect. Much of interest in the chapels is literally obscured. Head for the lighter cloister, and go in the afternoon, when the low light enters the façade's rose window.

🔘 A great place for a relaxed drink in the neighbourhood is Pois, Café *(see p60),* whose Austrian owners are helping to keep Alfama cosmopolitan.

- Largo da Sé
- Map G4
- 218 866 752
- Cloister: open 9am–7pm Mon–Sat, 2–5pm Sun. Adm €2.50 (concessions €1.25)
- Treasury: open 10am–5pm Mon–Sat. Adm €2.50 (concessions €1.25)

Top 10 Features

1. Rose Window
2. Belltowers
3. Romanesque Nave
4. Gothic Ambulatory Chapels
5. Capela de Bartolomeu Joanes
6. St Anthony's Font
7. Cloister
8. 13th-century Iron Railing
9. Archeological Finds
10. Treasury

1 Rose Window
Reconstructed using parts of the original, the rose window *(above left)* softens the façade's rather severe aspect, but unfortunately lets in only a limited amount of light.

2 Belltowers
These stocky towers – defining features of the Sé – echo those of Coimbra's cathedral, built a few years earlier by the same master builder, Frei Roberto. A taller third tower over the crossing collapsed in the 1755 earthquake *(see p32).*

3 Romanesque Nave
Little remains of the original cathedral beyond the renovated nave. It gives onto a chancel enclosed by an ambulatory, a 14th-century addition.

4 Gothic Ambulatory Chapels
The Chapel of São Cosme and São Damião is one of nine on the ambulatory. Look out for the tombs of nobleman Lopo Fernandes Pacheco *(above)* and his wife, Maria Villalobos.

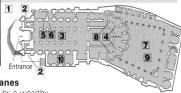

Entrance

Capela de Bartolomeu Joanes
This Gothic chapel, sponsored by a wealthy Lisbon merchant in 1324, contains the founder's tomb and the 15th-century Renaissance retable *(above)*, painted by Cristóvão de Figueiredo, Garcia Fernandes and Diogo de Contreiras.

St Anthony's Font
Tradition has it that Fernando Martins Bulhões (later St Anthony) was baptized in this font – which now bears a tile panel of the saint preaching to the fishes. He is also said to have had his early education at the cathedral school.

Cloister
The Gothic cloister, reached through one of the ambulatory's chapels, was an early addition to the Sé. Some of its decoration anticipates the Manueline style.

13th-century Iron Railing
One of the ambulatory chapels is closed off by a 13th-century iron railing *(left)*, the only one of its kind to survive in Portugal.

Archeological Finds
Remains left by Moors, Visigoths, Romans and Phoenicians have been found in the excavation of the cloister *(right)*.

Treasury
The first-floor Treasury is a museum of religious art, with some important holdings. Its most famous treasure, the relics of St Vincent *(see p32)*, was lost in the 1755 earthquake.

Fascinating finds from Lisbon's past
Archeologically, the Sé is a work in progress – as are the castle *(see pp8–9)* and many other parts of central Lisbon. What is most exciting about all this digging is that ever more ancient and striking remains are being uncovered. Public information can lag behind archeological breakthroughs – make a point of asking, and you may be treated to a glimpse of the latest find from Lisbon's past.

For more Lisbon places of worship See pp32–3

Museu Nacional de Arte Antiga

Lisbon's Museu Nacional de Arte Antiga is Portugal's national gallery, a treasure trove of historically illuminating art. Housed in a 17th-century palace that was built for the counts of Alvor, the museum was inaugurated in 1884 and today contains a vast collection of European art dating from the 14th to the 19th centuries, including the most complete collection of Portuguese works in the world. The museum's location, looking out over the river and the port area, gives it a delightfully enviable position.

Panels of St Vincent, detail

🌟 There is a lot to look at here. As with any large museum with a wide-ranging collection, study the layout and decide what to concentrate on. For 15 minutes with Nuno Gonçalves or Hieronymus Bosch, it may well be worth giving the world's largest collection of 18th-century French silverware a miss; or vice versa.

🍴 For lunch or dinner, an alternative to the museum restaurant is Nariz de Vinho Tinto, a short but steep climb up Rua do Conde opposite the museum (see p89).

- Rua das Janelas Verdes
- Map E5
- 213 912 800
- 10am–6pm Wed–Sun, 2–6pm Tue
- Admission €5 (concessions €2; under-14s free; free before 2pm Sun & public holidays)
- www.mnarteantiga-ipmuseus.pt

Top 10 Features

1 The Panels of St Vincent
2 The Temptations of St Anthony
3 St Jerome
4 St Augustine
5 Conversation
6 Chapel of St Albert
7 Namban Screens
8 Portuguese and Chinese Ceramics
9 Indo-Portuguese Furniture
10 Garden/Restaurant/Shop

1 The Panels of St Vincent
Arguably the most important Portuguese painting, this polyptych of around 1470 (probably by Nuno Gonçalves) portrays rich and poor in historically fascinating detail.

3 St Jerome
This unusual portrait (above) transcends the conventions of religious art. Painted in 1521 by Albrecht Dürer – who used a 93-year-old Antwerp man as his model – it is above all a portrayal of old age.

2 The Temptations of St Anthony
Hieronymous Bosch's three-panelled feast of fear and fantasy (above) is one of the museum's treasures – and one of the world's great paintings.

4 St Augustine
This mid-15th century work by Piero della Francesca was identified in 1946 as the missing panel of an altarpiece painted for the church of St Augustine in Borgo San Sepolcro, Italy. Note the crystal staff.

5 Conversation
Pieter de Hooch was a genre painter whose treatment of light was perhaps more complex than that of his contemporary, Vermeer. This work shows his key qualities as an artist.

 One of the figures depicted in the Panels of St Vincent is said to be the likely artist, Nuno Gonçalves.

Chapel of St Albert
Find your way to the annexe to see the restored chapel of the former Carmelite convent of Santo Alberto, decorated with blue and white *azulejos*.

Key

Third floor

Second floor

First floor

Ground floor

Namban Screens
After encountering Portuguese travellers in the 16th century, Japan's artists portrayed them as *namban-jin*, or "southern barbarians". The screens were not meant to be shown outside Japan.

Portuguese and Chinese Ceramics
The museum's 7,500-piece collection of ceramics illustrates the interplay of influences. From the 16th century, Portuguese faïence shows traces of Ming, while Chinese porcelain features coats of arms and other Portuguese motifs.

Indo-Portuguese Furniture
The most interesting of the museum's furniture collections is probably the group of Indo-Portuguese pieces. The *contadores* are many-drawered chests that combine orderliness on top with decorative abandon below.

Garden/Restaurant/Shop
The museum's downstairs restaurant gives onto a pleasant garden overlooking the river; upstairs is another café and a well-stocked gift shop.

La Nuit des Musées

If you are in Lisbon in May, visit this museum at night to enjoy a programme of concerts and other events – not least the guided midnight tours. Part of a Europe-wide French initiative to make museum visits more than Sunday afternoon outings, La Nuit des Musées gives access to the museum's treasures in a quite different context.

For more Lisbon museums See pp34–5

15

Parque das Nações

Built on the site of Lisbon's successful Expo 98 world exposition, held to mark the 500th anniversary of Vasco da Gama's epic voyage to India, the "Park of the Nations" is a new, self-contained riverside district east of the centre. It has Belém to it's west and showcases Portuguese architecture of a younger era. A bustling amusement park and trade-fair centre by day, by night the park becomes a concert and events venue, with a young nightlife scene and a casino. There's also an ambitious residential development.

Boardwalk

🌿 Early mornings in the Parque can be very refreshing, while summer afternoons are hotter, brighter and more humid here than in most other parts of the city. The undulating lawn area next to the Oceanário is a good spot for a rest, as are the benches along the riverfront.

🥤 Drinks can be bought at kiosks dotted around the Parque.

• Avenida Dom João II
• Map C2
• 218 919 898
• Oceanário: 218 917 002/06. Open 10am–8pm (7pm in winter) daily. Adm €12 (over-65s €6; children 4–12 €5.50; under-4s free). www.oceanario.pt
• Knowledge Pavilion – Ciência Viva: 218 917 100. Open 10am–6pm Tue–Fri, 11am–7pm Sat & Sun. Adm €7 (under-18s and over-65s €4; children 3–6 €3; under-3s free). www.pavconhecimento.pt

Top 10 Features

1. Oceanário
2. Portugal Pavilion
3. Knowledge Pavilion – Ciência Viva
4. Casino
5. Cable Car
6. Nautical Centre
7. Torre Vasco da Gama
8. Gardens
9. Restaurants
10. Shops

1 Oceanário

The world's second-largest aquarium *(above)* has hundreds of aquatic species organized by habitat and viewed on two levels. The vast central tank has species large and small, swimming round and round in uneasy peace. Impossibly cuddly-looking sea otters, in a side tank, get the most affection.

2 Portugal Pavilion

Impressive, with its concrete canopy suspended like a sail above its forecourt, the Portugal Pavilion was once going to house the Council of Ministers. There are plans to convert it into a museum and exhibition centre.

3 Knowledge Pavilion – Ciência Viva

This large, child-friendly science museum is full of interactive exhibits *(left)*, simulations, experiments and activities for various age groups, using cutting-edge technology and multimedia.

4 Casino

The latest addition to the Parque das Nações, in the former Future Pavilion, caters to all categories of gambler, with serried ranks of tinkling slot machines and green baize tables for poker, roulette and black jack.

Cable Car
Running most of the length of the Parque above the riverside, the cable car ride *(below)* gives an overview of the area and good views of the river and the Vasco da Gama bridge. If the breeze is up on the estuary, the cars may swing from side to side.

Nautical Centre
The Doca dos Olivais nautical centre rents out equipment for various water sports *(above)* and related activities.

Torre Vasco da Gama
At 145 m (476 ft), this is Lisbon's tallest building *(left)*, albeit removed from the rest of the urban sky-line. On a good day, views from the top extend as far as Setúbal. It is due to open as a hotel in 2011.

Gardens
Many of the rather anaemic-looking gardens planted for Expo 98 have grown into healthy patches of urban greenery. They now succeed in softening the concrete and steel, particularly along the waterfront *(below)*.

Restaurants
The wide range of over 40 waterfront restaurants, many with outdoor seating, are popular for weekend lunches *(below)*, but they are also an important part of the Parque das Nações nightlife scene.

Shops
Most shops are in the Vasco da Gama shopping centre, but retailing is developing elsewhere in the Parque. Electronics and interior decoration showrooms are now in operation, and when the FIL trade-fair area – formerly the Expo's national pavilions – puts on a consumer fair, plenty of customers turn up to see the latest offers.

Card Advantages
The Cartão do Parque costs €17.50 for adults and €9 for children and pensioners. It includes one free visit to the Oceanarium and Ciência Viva, one round-trip in a cable car, a ride on the mini-train, and discounts for bicycle hire. The Cartão do Parque is valid for one month. However, it can only be bought at the main visitors' kiosk located at the entrance.

TOP 10 Torre de Belém

The defensive tower at Belém is a jewel of the Manueline architectural style, combining Moorish, Renaissance and Gothic elements in a dazzling whole. It was built in 1515–20 by Francisco de Arruda, probably to a design by Diogo Boitac. At the time of its construction, the tower stood on an island in the river Tejo, about 200 m (650 ft) from the northern riverbank, and so commanded the approach to Lisbon more fully than it does today. The land between the tower and the Jerónimos monastery has since been reclaimed from the river.

Portuguese coat of arms

🕐 The tower is at its prettiest in the early morning or late afternoon. Tour groups tend to go early, so go as late as you can for a quieter visit.

🍴 Nearby restaurants (including Vela Latina – *see p85*) often fill up quickly; if you can't find a table here, cross the railway line by the footbridge and walk to the nearby Centro Cultural de Belém *(see p86)* and the pleasant Jardim das Oliveiras outdoor café.

• Avda Brasilia
• Map A6
• 213 620 034
• Open 10am–5pm (6pm May–Sep) Tue–Sun
• Admission €5 (concessions €1.50; senior citizens €3; under-14s free; free 10am–2pm Sun & public hols)
• www.igespar.pt

Top 10 Features

1. Battlements
2. Renaissance Loggia
3. Governor's Room
4. Dungeon
5. Watchtowers
6. Virgin and Child Sculpture
7. Rhinoceros Detail
8. Manueline Details
9. Armillary Spheres
10. Exhibitions

Battlements
The merlons of most of the tower's battlements are decorated with the cross of the Order of Christ, carved to look like features on a shield. The smaller merlons at the rear and on top of the tower are crowned with pyramid-shaped spikes.

Renaissance Loggia
An arcaded loggia overlooks the main deck – comparisons to a ship are unavoidable here. The loggia breaks with the military style of most of the building and adds a theatrical element, while the railing and tracery of the balustrade *(right)* are pure Manueline. Balconies on each side of the tower echo the loggia's style.

Governor's Room
Now empty, this room *(left)* is where the tower's first governor, Gaspar de Paiva, discharged his duties. After it became obsolete, lighthouse keepers and customs officials worked here. The room's acoustics amplify the slightest whisper.

➤ *Lovers of the nautical and military should visit Museu da Marinha in Belém (see p84) and Museu Militar by Santa Apolónia station.*

4 Dungeon
From the tower's vaulted bottom level – also used as a dungeon – 16 cannon covered the approaches to Lisbon.

5 Watchtowers
You can't miss the Moorish-influenced watchtowers *(below)*. Their domes are seated on Manueline rope-like circles and rise to a pile of small spheres reminiscent of the tops of chess pieces.

7 Rhinoceros Detail
Each of the sentry boxes is supported by a naturalistically carved stone. The rhinoceros at the base of the north-western box is the most famous, as it is thought to be the first European stone representation of this animal. Time and the weather have rounded its features, however.

6 Virgin and Child Sculpture
A statue of Our Lady of Safe Homecoming stands by the light well that was used to lower cannon into the dungeon. She evokes not only the intrepid explorers of Portugal's past, but also everyday sailors – and a concern for absent husbands and sons that is one of the roots of the longing of *saudade*.

Holy Namesake
Belém means Bethlehem – and the name is taken from a chapel dedicated to St Mary of Bethlehem, built in the mid-15th century near the river's edge in what was then Restelo. This chapel subsequently gave way to the grand Jerónimos church and monastery; the church is still known as Santa Maria de Belém. The name Restelo, for its part, now applies to the area above and behind Belém, a leafy district of fine residences and embassy buildings.

8 Manueline Details
Ropes and knots were the main theme for the Manueline masons here. The tracery of some of the balustrades features the near-organic shapes *(right)* that would be developed in later Manueline buildings.

9 Armillary Spheres
The armillary spheres carved above the loggia were instruments for showing the motion of the stars around the earth. They became a symbol of Portugal, and still feature on the national flag.

10 Exhibitions
The tower's former dungeon, now quite bright, is often used for temporary exhibitions, as well as for a permanent information display for visitors and a gift shop.

The Manueline style is named after Dom Manuel I (known as The Fortunate), who was king at the height of the era of discovery.

🔟 Museu Nacional do Azulejo

Ceramic tiles, or azulejos, are a distinctive aspect of Portuguese culture, featuring in contexts both mundane and sacred. The art of making them is a Moorish inheritance, much adapted – most noticeably in the addition of human figurative motifs, which Islam forbids. This museum dedicated to tiles is enjoyable both for the excellent displays and for its beautiful setting, a 16th-century convent transformed over the centuries to include some of the city's prettiest cloisters and one of its most richly decorated churches.

Portuguese "carpet" tiles

⭐ The rather awkward location of the Tile Museum can be turned into an asset if you combine it with a visit to Parque das Nações *(see p16– 17)*, a shopping trip to Santa Apolónia *(see p41)*, or lunch at D'Avis *(see p61)*.

⭐ The best place for a pleasant drink in this neighbourhood is the museum's own cafeteria; otherwise, head for Santa Apolónia *(see p41)*.

- Rua da Madre de Deus 4
- Map C2
- 218 100 340
- Open 2–6pm Tue; 10am–6pm Wed–Sun
- Admission €5
- http://mnazulejo. imc-ip.pt

Top 10 Features

1. Lisbon Panel
2. Moorish Tiles
3. Manueline Cloister
4. Madre de Deus Church
5. Nossa Senhora da Vida Altarpiece
6. Renaissance Cloister
7. Tile-making Exhibit
8. Temporary Exhibitions
9. Shop
10. Cafeteria and Winter Garden

Moorish Tiles

With their attractive geometrical patterns, varied colour palettes, and glazing techniques, Moorish tiles continue to be an inspiration to tile-makers and home decorators alike.

Manueline Cloister

This small but stunning cloister *(above)* is one of the few surviving features of the original convent of Madre de Deus. This is the Manueline style at its most restrained. The geometrical wall tiles were added in the 17th century.

Lisbon Panel

On the second floor of the main cloister and 23 m (75 ft) long, this vast tiled panorama of Lisbon *(below)* is a captivating depiction of the city's waterfront as it looked in about 1740, before the great earthquake. It was transferred here from one of the city's palaces.

Madre de Deus Church

The magnificent barrel-vaulted convent church is the result of three centuries of construction and decoration *(left)*, and contains enough paintings to fill a gallery. Today's layout dates from the 16th century. The tile panels are from the 17th and 18th, as is the Baroque gilt woodwork and other expressions of wealth.

Renaissance Cloister

Part of the first major alterations to the convent in the 16th century, this airy, simple cloister on two levels *(below)* is the work of Diogo de Torralva. Now glassed in to protect collections and visitors alike from extremes of weather, it remains the light heart of the building.

Nossa Senhora da Vida Altarpiece

Almost 5 m (16 ft) square and containing over 1,000 tiles, this 16th-century Renaissance altarpiece by Marçal de Matos *(above)* shows the *Adoration of the Shepherds*, flanked by St Luke and St John.

Entrance

Key

	Second floor
	First floor
	Ground floor

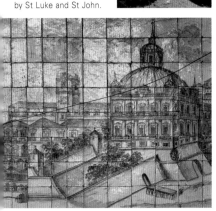

Tile-making Exhibit

Step-by-step exhibits of tile-making, from a lump of clay to the final glazing, help visitors to see how the medium combines practical uses with decorative ends.

A Nod from the 19th Century

When the southern façade of the church was restored in the late 19th century, the architect used as his model a painting, part of the Retábulo de Santa Auta, now in the Museu de Arte Antiga *(see pp14–15)*. This shows the convent and church as they looked in the early 16th century. Indoors, the quest for authenticity was less zealous. In one of the cloisters, 19th-century restorers have left a potent symbol of their own era: an image of a steam locomotive, incorporated into one of the upper-level capitals.

Temporary Exhibitions

The ground and first floors are devoted to temporary exhibitions – like contemporary tile art, an important category in Portugal.

Shop

A large selection of quality reproductions of classic tile designs are available, as well as modern tiles and other gift items.

Cafeteria and Winter Garden

Suitably tiled with food-related motifs *(left)*, the museum cafeteria is worth a light lunch stop or a coffee. The courtyard is partly covered and acts as a winter garden.

🔟 Palácio de Queluz

Queluz is like a miniature Versailles – an exquisite Rococo palace with formal gardens and parkland, just 15 minutes from central Lisbon. Prince Pedro, younger son of Dom João V, had it built as a summer palace in 1747–52. Thirteen years later, when he married his niece the future Dona Maria I, he commissioned Jean-Baptiste Robillon to design extensions to make it the permanent royal residence. Queluz had a brief golden era before the royal family fled to Brazil after Napoleon's invasion in 1807.

Statue of sphinx in garden

🐾 An early-morning visit to Queluz can be usefully combined with a trip to Sintra *(see pp26–7)*, but remember that Sintra's national palace is closed on Wednesdays, unlike other monuments and museums.

📍 The terrace at the Pousada is easily the best place for a drink – unless you have an invitation to an event in the palace itself.

- Largo do Palácio
- Map A1
- 214 343 860
- Open 9am–5pm Wed–Mon (gardens to 6pm May–Sep)
- Admission €7 (concessions €2.50; under-14s free); gardens only €3

Top 10 Features

1. Gardens
2. Robillon Pavilion
3. Don Quixote Chamber
4. Lion Staircase
5. Sala dos Embaixadores
6. Corredor das Mangas
7. Chapel
8. Music Room
9. Throne Room
10. Cozinha Velha and Pousada Dona Maria I

Gardens

Two formal gardens, the Neptune Garden and Malta Garden, fill the space between the palace's two asymmetric wings. Laid out by a French architect, they contain fountains, statues and topiary.

Lion Staircase

This beautifully flowing staircase *(above)* links the lower parkland area to the palace and formal gardens. It is flanked by an arcaded "dwarf gallery" with a water cascade flowing into a tiled canal; here, the royal family went boating.

Robillon Pavilion

This warmly pink building *(left)*, replete with windows, balustrades and pillars, is a bit too fussy and overloaded for purists. It was designed by French architect Robillon.

Don Quixote Chamber

The inlaid circular-pattern floor and domed ceiling make this square room *(below)* look round. It is named for painted scenes from *Don Quixote*.

5 Sala dos Embaixadores

The magnificent Ambassadors' Room *(below)* was used for diplomatic audiences, and is opulently decorated with stucco work and painted and gilded carved woodwork. The *trompe l'oeil* ceiling depicts the royal family at a concert, for which purpose the room was also used.

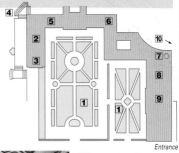

Entrance

6 Corredor das Mangas

The hallway linking the old and newer parts of Queluz was named for the glass cylinders, or sleeves *(mangas)*, of its candles. It is also called the *Corredor dos Azulejos*, after its painted wall tiles *(below)*.

7 Chapel

The chapel was the first part of the palace to be completed, in 1752. It was also used for concerts, some by Dona Maria I's own chamber orchestra. She and her sisters are said to have painted some of the wall panels.

8 Music Room

The Music Room *(left)* was used for concerts and even opera performances, and doubled as a venue for important christenings. It still acts as a concert venue.

9 Throne Room

Competing in grandeur with the Ambassadors' Room, and with a magnificent oval, domed ceiling, the Throne Room also served as ballroom, church and theatre – and for lying-in-state.

10 Cozinha Velha and Pousada Dona Maria I

The old palace kitchens have long housed the fine Cozinha Velha restaurant *(right)*. The newer Pousada Dona Maria I, in the former quarters of the Royal Guard, is as close as you'll get to living at Queluz.

The Wailing Queen

Dona Maria I, after she became queen and then lost a son, famously lost her mind. Visitors described hearing her wailing as she wandered the corridors of Queluz. She was exiled to Brazil in 1807 with her younger son, then Regent, to escape the invasion led by the French Emperor Napoleon.

For details of Pousada Dona Maria I **See p114**

🔟 Museu Calouste Gulbenkian

Based on the private collections of oil millionaire Calouste Gulbenkian, this museum spans over 4,000 years of art history while remaining marvellously manageable for the visitor. Internationally recognized for the quality of its collections and premises, the museum is part of an attractive 1960s complex that houses the headquarters of the Calouste Gulbenkian Foundation and also includes a concert hall and auditoria for its orchestra and choir, an art library, a peaceful park and a modern art museum.

Statue of Calouste Gulbenkian

🕐 Taking in another museum in one day might be pushing it, but the Centro de Arte Moderna José Azeredo Perdigão – also part of the Gulbenkian Foundation – has a good collection of contemporary Portuguese art, and stages frequent temporary shows.

🍴 There are good cafés at both museums.

• Avenida de Berna 45A
• Map F1
• 217 823 000
• Open 10am–5:45pm Tue–Sun
• Admission €4; ticket to both museums €7 (children free, 50 per cent discount for students and over-65s; free on Sun) • www.museu.gulbenkian.pt

Top 10 Features

1. 3rd-dynasty Egyptian Bowl
2. 5thC BC Greek Vase
3. Oriental Islamic Art
4. Yüan Dynasty Stem Cup
5. Portrait of an Old Man
6. St Catherine and St Joseph
7. Louis XV and XVI furniture
8. Boy Blowing Bubbles
9. Diana Statue
10. Lalique collection

1 3rd-dynasty Egyptian Bowl
Found in a tomb north of Thebes, this simple, elegant alabaster bowl was modelled on an everyday ointment bowl. The ancient Egyptians adorned tombs with such copies of everyday objects made from noble materials. This one is 4,000 years old.

2 5thC BC Greek Vase
This beautiful, wide-rimmed terracotta vase *(right)* is decorated with mythological motifs: the abduction of Phoebe and Hilaira by Castor and Pollux, and a bacchanalian scene.

3 Oriental Islamic Art
A large gallery shows a wide-ranging collection of manuscripts, carpets *(right)*, textiles, ceramics and other objects from Turkey, Syria, the Caucasus (including Gulbenkian's birthplace Armenia), Persia and India.

4 Yüan Dynasty Stem Cup
This rare blue-glazed piece dates from an earlier period (1279–1368) than most of the Far Eastern collection. It is decorated with delicate high-relief cutouts of Taoist figures under bamboo leaves.

Sign up for DK's email newsletter on traveldk.com

5 Portrait of an Old Man

This engaging *chiaroscuro* portrait of a bearded man *(left)* is an example of Rembrandt's preoccupation at that time with ageing. The gaze is tired, and the large hands intricately lined but held in a relaxed manner. Nothing is known about the model.

6 St Catherine and St Joseph

Two paintings by the 15th-century Flemish master Rogier van der Weyden are believed to be parts of an altarpiece; a third element is in London's National Gallery. The female figure *(below)* is thought to be St Catherine of Alexandria.

9 Diana Statue

A graceful marble 1780 statue *(right)* by the French sculptor Jean-Antoine Houdon is unusual for the era in that it depicts the goddess in movement, and completely naked. It belonged to Catherine the Great of Russia and was exhibited at the Hermitage, where its nudity caused scandal and notoriety.

Entrance

7 Louis XV and XVI Furniture

Considered ostentatious and over-decorated by some, the 18th-century French pieces *(above)* in the decorative art collection fascinate for their materials and craftsmanship. Stars include a Louis XV chest inlaid with Japanese lacquer panels, gold leaf, mother-of-pearl, bronze and ebony; and a table with folding flaps and a shelf that flips over to reveal a mirror.

8 Boy Blowing Bubbles

Édouard Manet's 1867 painting *(main picture)* is not just a version of the popular allegory on the transience of life and art, but a deftly and freely painted portrait of Léon-Édouard Koëlla, Manet's stepson.

10 Lalique Collection

Gulbenkian was a close friend of the French Art Nouveau jeweller René Lalique, and bought many of his graceful pieces. In fact, this part of the museum has almost too many.

The Spoils of Oil

Calouste Sarkis Gulbenkian was an Armenian who made a huge fortune negotiating the transfer of assets between oil companies – each time earning a five per cent commission. He came to Lisbon during World War II, staying at the Hotel Aviz until his death in 1955. His will stipulated that a foundation be set up in Portugal to care for his vast collection and to support the arts.

TOP 10 Sintra

Recognized in 1995 as a UNESCO World Heritage Site, Sintra was the summer retreat of Portuguese kings from the 13th to the late 19th centuries. It still possesses many of the classic qualities of a hill station: a cooler climate than the city, ample greenery and an atmosphere conducive to indulging romantic whims. The older town is pretty but crowded, and the surrounding landscapes and sights are an essential part of any visit. Access from Lisbon is straightforward, by motorway or by train from Rossio Station.

Window, Palácio Nacional

🌀 Sintra's romantic and refreshing qualities may be seriously challenged on summer weekends, when tour groups and locals collide in the square in front of the Palácio Nacional. Go during the week, and avoid the middle of the day in summer.

🍹 Bars and cafés in the old town fill up quickly and charge inflated prices. For a different atmosphere, walk past the Tourist Office to Lawrence's Hotel *(see p116)* and have a drink in one of its small, colonial-cosy public rooms.

• Tourist information: Praça da República 23, Sintra. 219 231 157 www.cm-sintra.pt
• Sintra lies 30 km (18 miles) northwest of Lisbon. Trains run frequently from Lisbon's Rossio and Entrecampos Station.

Top 10 Features

1. Palácio Nacional de Sintra
2. Castelo dos Mouros
3. Palácio Nacional da Pena
4. Parque da Pena
5. Quinta da Regaleira
6. Parque da Liberdade
7. Museu do Brinquedo
8. São Pedro Market
9. Palácio de Seteais
10. Monserrate

2 Castelo dos Mouros
The 8th-century castle *(above)* seems to hover above the town between boulder-littered crags. It was captured from the Moors by Afonso Henriques in 1147. Dom Fernando II partially rebuilt it in the 19th century. Inside are a ruined chapel and a Moorish cistern.

1 Palácio Nacional de Sintra
Twin chimneys mark the former royal palace *(below)*. Begun in the 14th century and extended in the 16th, it is a captivating mix of styles from Moorish to Baroque.

3 Palácio Nacional da Pena
Dom Fernando II, Dona Maria II's German-born king consort, had this fabulous toyland palace *(left)* built in the mid-19th century. The work of a hyperactive imagination, it exhibits all his eclectic tastes, and has been preserved as it was when the royal family lived there.

4 Parque da Pena

Filled with exotic trees and shrubs, the park around the Palácio da Pena is another of Dom Fernando II's contributions to Sintra's romantic magic. It contains the chalet he had built for his mistress, a German opera singer whom he later married.

Estefânia

5 Quinta da Regaleira

This lavish palace *(left)* looms up on a steep bend in the old road to Sintra. It was built around 1900 for António Augusto Carvalho Monteiro, an eccentric millionaire. He was a bibliophile and keen dabbler in alchemy and other esoteric subjects.

6 Parque da Liberdade

The tree-thronged town park with a variety of tree species and steep steps and paths occupies the top of the valley below the old town.

7 Museu do Brinquedo

One man's extensive toy collection from the 1930s on *(above)* is housed in the old fire station. It has a toy restoration workshop and a small shop.

The Artist King

Ferdinand Saxe-Coburg-Gotha was known in Portugal as Dom Fernando II, the "artist" king. Like his cousin Prince Albert, who married the English Queen Victoria, he loved art, nature and the new inventions of the time. He was himself a watercolour painter. Ferdinand enthusiastically adopted his new country and devoted his life to patronizing the arts. His lifelong dream of building the extravagant Palace of Pena was completed in 1885, the year he died.

8 São Pedro Market

Antiques are a feature of the lively market held in the suburb of São Pedro on the second and fourth Sundays of each month.

9 Palácio de Seteais

Built in 1787, Seteais (now a hotel) got its neo-classical façade later. It's best to visit, well dressed, for tea or a meal.

10 Monserrate

The beautiful gardens of Monserrate, with their fantastic Moorish-style palace *(right)* and exotic plants, were laid out by English residents.

 English poet Lord Byron, an early visitor to Monserrate, extolled the beauty of the place in his Childe Harold's Pilgrimage.

Left **Lisbon recaptured, 1147** Centre **Monument to the Restoration** Right **Birth of the Republic**

🔟 Moments in History

1 138 BC: Roman Occupation

Although they had reached the Iberian peninsula in the second century BC, the Romans did not conquer its westernmost parts until nearly a century later. The trading post of Olisipo, Lisbon's Greek name (sometimes associated with Ulysses), was occupied in 138 BC.

2 714: Moorish Occupation

Roman Lisbon was invaded by Alan tribes from the north, about whom little is known, and then by the Visigoths, who ruled from Toledo. Less than three centuries after the end of Roman rule, however, the Visigoths were swept from power by Moorish armies crossing into Iberia at the Straits of Gibraltar. Lisbon fell to the Moors in 714.

3 1147: Reconquest

The Christian reconquest of the Iberian peninsula from the Moors began in the north, where Afonso Henriques founded the Portuguese kingdom – as distinct from the future Spanish kingdom of León – in 1140. His armies reached Lisbon in 1147 and took the city following a three-month seige.

Tomb of Vasco da Gama

4 1497: Vasco da Gama Sails from Belém

The crowning achievement of Portugal's era of discovery and expansion was Vasco da Gama's well-documented, nearly year-long voyage to India. Rounding the Cape of Good Hope, he proved Columbus wrong and gave the Portuguese the competitive edge in the spice trade.

5 1640: Independence from Spain

Spain had usurped the Portuguese throne in 1581, after the death of Dom Sebastião and much of the Portuguese nobility in an ill-conceived military adventure in north Africa. The 1640 coup at Lisbon's royal palace reinstated self-rule and proclaimed the Duke of Bragança king of Portugal.

6 1755: The Great Earthquake

On 1 November 1755, All Saints' Day, a massive earthquake struck southern Portugal and laid waste to central Lisbon. Three shocks were followed by fires and tidal waves. The scale of the destruction shocked the world.

7 1910: Portugal Becomes a Republic

In 1908, Dom Carlos and his heir were assassinated by republican activists in Terreiro do Paço. The king's surviving son became Dom Manuel II, but abdicated in October 1910 in the face of a republican revolution. The Republic was formalized on 5 October.

 Preceding pages **Padrão dos Descobrimentos (Monument to the Discoveries), western face** *(see p84)*

Rescue of an earthquake survivor

1933: The New State

António de Oliveira Salazar, who had been appointed finance minister in the hope that he could solve the country's financial crisis, was asked to form a government in 1932. The following year his new constitution was passed by parliament, in effect making him an authoritarian dictator.

1974: The Carnation Revolution

Salazar's successor Marcelo Caetano and his government were overthrown in a virtually bloodless coup by a group of army captains on 25 April. Three men were killed by shots coming from the headquarters of the PIDE, the political police, as crowds outside cheered the end of its reign of fear.

1986: European Union Membership

After a few tumultuous years following the 1974 revolution, stable democracy was established in Portugal. Independence had already been restored to most of the colonies and Portugal was now ready to turn to Europe. Membership brought a welcome boost to the economy, in the form of both subsidies and foreign investment.

Top 10 Historical Figures

1 Viriato
The legendary leader of the Lusitanians, a Celtic-Iberian tribe that resisted Roman occupation for two decades.

2 Tariq
As Berber leader of the Moorish force, Tariq conquered most of the Iberian peninsula in 711–16.

3 Afonso Henriques
Having taken control of the countship of Portucale, Afonso was calling himself "Portucalense king" by 1140.

4 Henry the Navigator
Son of Dom João, Prince Henry was the architect of Portugal's early overseas expansion in the 15th century.

5 Duke of Bragança
Hesitant at first, he soon agreed to be king, as Dom João IV, after the 1640 coup.

6 Marquis of Pombal
Chief minister under Dom José I, he reconstructed the city after the earthquake, but was later reviled as a despot.

7 Eça de Queiroz
The 19th-century chronicler of Lisbon was a member of the Cenáculo, a group of writers opposed to the monarchy.

8 António de Oliveira Salazar
Portugal's deceptively low-key dictator was originally a professor of economics.

9 Mário Soares
The first democratically elected post-revolution prime minister won a second term and, in 1986, the presidency.

10 Aníbal Cavaco Silva
Leader of the Social Democrats and prime minister from 1985 to 1995, he was elected president in 2005.

The Museu da Sociedade Geográfica (see p66) is full of booty and memorabilia from Portugal's colonial era.

Left **Cloister, Mosteiro dos Jerónimos** Right **Igreja do Carmo**

Churches and Monasteries

Mosteiro dos Jerónimos
The country's most important monument displays the exuberant, almost oriental ornamentation that is a chief characteristic of the Manueline style *(see pp10–11)*.

Sé Catedral
Seen at a distance, Lisbon's cathedral can almost conjure up the mosque that preceded it. Up close, the Romanesque building is attractively simple *(see pp12–13)*.

Igreja de Santa Engrácia
One of Lisbon's most uplifting churches is an unmistakable feature of the city's eastern skyline. This Baroque beauty is most famous for having taken 284 years to build, but it also houses the cenotaphs to national heroes, hence the groups of schoolchildren clustered around. **Tomb of Maria I, Basílica da Estrela**
✆ *Campo de Santa Clara • Map R3*
• 10am–5pm Tue–Sun • Adm charge

Igreja de São Domingos
One of Lisbon's oldest churches is one of its hardiest survivors. Built in 1242, it was damaged by earthquakes in 1531 and 1755, and ravaged by fire in 1959. The blackened interior helps you imagine the days when Inquisition processions would begin here, to end with charred corpses. ✆ *Largo de São Domingos*
• Map M3 • 8am–7pm daily • Free

Igreja do Carmo
The late 14th-century church and convent of Carmo was one of Lisbon's main places of worship before the roof caved in on All Saints' Day 1755, killing the congregation. The evocative ruin, with its bare Gothic arches, now houses an archaeological museum. ✆ *Largo do Carmo • Map L4*
• 10am–7pm Mon–Sat (Oct–Apr: 10am–6pm) • Adm charge

Basílica da Estrela
This domed Lisbon landmark was built from 1779 to give thanks for the birth of a son and male heir to Dona Maria I. Sadly, the boy died of smallpox before the church was finished. Inside is the queen's tomb, and a nativity scene with over 500 cork-and-terracotta figures; ask the sacristan to show you it. ✆ *Praça da Estrela • Map E4*
• 7:45am–8pm daily • Free

São Vicente de Fora
In 1173, when St Vincent was proclaimed patron saint of Portugal, his relics were moved from the Algarve to the original church on this site. Philip II of Spain had the present Mannerist church built in the early 17th century. As if to prove a point about independence, in 1885 the refectory was turned into the pantheon of the Bragança royal family. ✆ *Largo de São Vicente*
• Map Q3 • 10am–5pm Tue–Sun • Free

Among Lisbon's working monasteries is Convento dos Cardeais in Rua do Século.

8 Igreja de Santo António

Lisbon's patron saint was allegedly born here (as Fernando Bulhões) in the late 12th century. The present Baroque church replaced the one lost to the 1755 earthquake. In June, weddings are held here, as St Anthony is said to bring luck to newly-weds.
◈ *Largo de Santo António à Sé*
• *Map N4* • *8am–7pm daily* • *Free*

Chapel of St John the Baptist, São Roque

9 Igreja de São Roque

Built in the 16th century for the Jesuit order, this church is famous for its opulent interior, particularly the Chapel of St John the Baptist. Made in Rome using lapis lazuli, agate, alabaster, amethyst, precious marbles, gold and silver, it was blessed by the pope, taken apart and sent to Lisbon in three ships. ◈ *Largo Trindade Coelho*
• *Map K3* • *9am–6pm Tue, Wed & Fri–Sun; 2–6pm Mon; 9am–9pm Thu* • *Free*

10 Igreja da Graça

The Augustinian monastery here dates from 1271, but was rebuilt after the 1755 earthquake. The church is home to the *Senhor dos Passos*, a figure of Christ bearing the cross, which is carried in a traditional procession at Lent.
◈ *Largo da Graça* • *Map P2* • *9:30am–12:30pm, 3–6pm Tue–Sat; 5–8pm Sun* • *Free*

Top 10 Manueline Gems

1 Torre de Belém
While more decorative than defensive today, this tower is a perfect Manueline gem.

2 Jerónimos Cloister
João de Castilho's cloister features the whole Manueline arsenal. Take your time in it.

3 South Portal of Jerónimos
This riot of decoration – saints, royals and symbols – is actually completely symmetrical.

4 Nave of Jerónimos
Mixing organic elements with geometry, octagonal piers encrusted with carvings rise to the web-like vaulting.

5 Conceição Velha Portal
The Manueline portal is the only remnant of the original 16th-century church, destroyed in the 1755 earthquake.

6 Portal, Museu do Azulejo
The Manueline portal dates from the 19th century, when the façade was reconstructed from a 16th-century painting.

7 Manueline Cloister, Museu do Azulejo
This small, attractive and relatively restrained cloister is a reminder of the building's 16th-century role as a convent.

8 Ermida de São Jerónimo
This simple chapel from 1514 gives the Manueline a broader, more contemporary aesthetic.

9 Casa dos Bicos
Built as a private palace in 1523, this structure picked up on Italian style as well as including Manueline windows.

10 Rossio Station
A nostalgic Neo-Manueline look back from 1892, with a hint of parallels to Art Nouveau.

The early 16th-century Manueline style is an exuberant architectural hybrid of Gothic with Spanish, Flemish and Italian elements.

33

Left **Lalique glass, Museu Calouste Gulbenkian** Centre **Museu Nacional do Azulejo** Right **CCB**

Museums and Galleries

1 Museu Calouste Gulbenkian

The Armenian oil baron and art collector Calouste Gulbenkian is arguably the single most important person in Portuguese post-war cultural life. His museum is a rare treat because it covers so much in such a manageable way – and also because it has pleasant gardens and a good contemporary arts centre *(see pp24–5)*.

2 Museu Nacional de Arte Antiga

Arguably the most important art museum in the country, Portugal's national museum provides a home for some priceless national and international works, including painting, sculpture, textiles and decorative art. It is sometimes referred to as the Museu das Janelas Verdes due to the building's green windows *(see pp14–15)*.

The Panels of St Vincent, Museu Nacional de Arte Antiga

3 Museu Nacional do Azulejo

Lisbon's tile museum is a tourist favourite, for good reason. It is housed in a stunning convent and church, covers tiles and tile-making comprehensively, and has the bonus of a pleasant café-restaurant *(see pp20–21)*.

4 Museu Nacional dos Coches

A coach museum is the sort of place you might not go to if you didn't have a special interest in the subject. In this case, that would be a mistake. This is one of Lisbon's most highly regarded and popular museums, for its collection of 52 horse-drawn coaches and the connections they create with the past. Ⓢ *Praça Afonso de Albuquerque • Map B6 • 213 610 850 • 10am–6pm Tue–Sun • Adm charge • www.museu doscoches-ipmuseus.pt*

5 Museu Colecção Berardo Arte Moderna e Contemporânea

One of the world's largest and richest collections of modern art was accumulated by business mogul José Berardo. The museum boasts about 1,000 works, from canvas and sculpture to video installations. Ⓢ *Praça do Império • Map B6 • 213 612 878 • 10am–7pm daily (to 10pm Sat) • Free • www.museuberardo.pt*

6 Galeria 111

With over 40 years in the business to its credit, this uptown gallery shows such artists as Paula Rego, Júlio Pomar and Joana Vasconcelos. Ⓢ *Campo Grande 113A • off map • 217 977 418 • 10am–7pm Tue–Sat • Free*

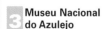

7 Zé dos Bois
ZDB, as it is also known, has consistently been Lisbon's most inspirational and genuinely "alternative" gallery. It is also a Bairro Alto bar. ⌖ Rua da Barroca 59 • Map K4 • 213 430 205 • 3–11pm Wed–Sat • Adm charge • www.zedosbois.org

8 Museu do Chiado
Guardian of Portuguese modernity in art, this museum has a collection beginning with Romanticism in the mid-19th century and extending throughout the 20th century, though the latter half is less fully covered. There are also temporary exhibitions and a pleasant courtyard café-restaurant (see p71).

9 Culturgest
The arts-patronage arm of a bank is one of Lisbon's most active cultural centres, focusing on modern music, dance, cinema, theatre and art. ⌖ Caixa Geral de Depósitos, Rua Arco do Cego • Map G1 • 217 905 155 • Galleries: 11am–7pm Mon & Wed–Fri; 2–8pm Sat & Sun • Adm charge • www.culturgest.pt

10 Fundação/Museu Arpad Szenes-Vieira da Silva
This museum is devoted to the work of Portuguese Modernist Maria Helena Vieira da Silva and her Hungarian husband, Arpad Szenes. ⌖ Praça das Amoreiras 56–8 • Map F3 • 213 880 044 • 10am–6pm Mon & Wed–Sun • Adm charge (free on Sun until 2pm) • www.fasvs.pt

Ornate coach, Museu Nacional dos Coches

Top 10 Portuguese Artists

1 Nuno Gonçalves
He is believed to be the 15th-century painter of The Panels of St Vincent, which may contain his self-portrait.

2 Grão Vasco (Vasco Fernandes)
One of Portugal's best-known 16th-century painters (c.1475–1542) is known for his Flemish-style altarpieces.

3 Josefa de Óbidos
This painter and engraver (1630–84) falls between the Mannerist and the Baroque.

4 Joaquim Machado de Castro
This celebrated sculptor (1731–1822) is best known for his equestrian statue of Dom José I in Praça do Comércio.

5 José Malhoa
A naturalistic painter (1855–1933), creator of the deliciously languorous O Fado.

6 Columbano Bordalo Pinheiro
A gifted portraitist, Columbano (1857–1929) painted many of the leading figures of the Republican movement.

7 Júlio Pomar
One of the country's essential 20th-century painters, Pomar (b.1926) was at odds with the Fascist dictatorship.

8 Paula Rego
Rego (b.1935) paints the Portuguese with rare acuity and beauty.

9 João Cutileiro
Portugal's best-known living sculptor (b.1937) has a knack for making marble playful.

10 Joana Vasconcelos
A master of transformation, Vasconcelos (b.1971) creates beauty from mundane items.

 Agenda Cultural (see p107) is the best guide to current exhibitions (in Portuguese only).

Left **View of the Castelo from Senhora do Monte** Centre **Cristo Rei** Right **Igreja da Graça**

🔟 City Views

1 Castelo
The view from under the umbrella pines on the Castle's esplanade takes in Alfama, the Baixa, Bairro Alto on the hill opposite, and the river. The light here is particularly warm in the late afternoon, encouraging you to linger. ◈ *Map N3*

2 Santa Luzia
Most tourists head for the nearby Largo das Portas do Sol viewpoint, on the other side of the Santa Luzia church. But this one has all the proper trappings, including a pergola with tiled pillars, walls and benches forming a veranda for the view. There's a café below, but it doesn't have the view. ◈ *Map P4*

Santa Luzia

3 São Pedro de Alcântara
This small garden is one of Lisbon's best known viewpoints. Bougainvillea tumbles onto the next terrace, a more formal and less accessible garden. The view extends across Restauradores and the Baixa to the Sé and the Castle. ◈ *Map K2*

4 Miradouro de Santa Catarina
Not just a visual vantage point, this is also a place to meet and hang out. Adamastor, the mythical creature from Camões' epic poem *The Lusiads*, presides over events from a stone plinth. There's a wide view of the river, the station at Cais do Sodré, the Alcântara docks and the 25 de Abril bridge. ◈ *Map J5*

5 Igreja da Graça
The pine-shaded esplanade by the Graça church has a café with a classic view of the lower city, the river and the bridge. Like the Castle's viewpoint, this one is best visited in the late afternoon. ◈ *Map P2*

6 Senhora do Monte
One of the highest vantage points in the city, Our Lady of the Mount (there is a small chapel behind the viewpoint) affords a grand vista that includes the Castle, the Graça church and the Mouraria quarter, as well as the Tejo estuary, the lower city, midtown Lisbon and the Monsanto park. ◈ *Map N1*

Wander around neighbourhoods such as Lapa and Alfama, and you'll soon find your own viewpoints.

The view from Castelo

Elevador de Santa Justa
The best close-up overview of the Baixa and Rossio, with the Castle above, is to be had from the terrace at the top of the Elevador de Santa Justa. It is reached via an extremely tight spiral staircase, but it is worth the climb just for the view. ⊗ Map M4

Cristo Rei
From his tall perch on the south side of the river, Christ the King spreads his arms to protect Lisbon. The 28-m (92-ft) statue on an 82-m (270-ft) pedestal was inaugurated in 1959 in thanks for Portugal's escape from involve-ment in World War II. Dubbed "the traffic policeman" when the traffic jams on the bridge were at their worst, the monument is a great vantage point for taking in all of Lisbon and the Tejo estuary. Lifts ascend to the platform beneath the statue. ⊗ off map

Jardim do Torel
The Jardim do Torel is a less well known viewpoint in a small garden on a slope overlooking Restauradores and the Avenida da Liberdade – providing not just a fine view but a great place for quiet contemplation too. ⊗ Map L1

Parque Eduardo VII
It's difficult to feel any real affection for Eduardo VII park, with its formal plan, its football-killing slope and its lack of shade, but climb to the top and you will see the architect's idea, as Lisbon stretches away from you in an unbroken perspective right down to the river. The sides offer a less commanding view but more shade and human interest. ⊗ Map F2

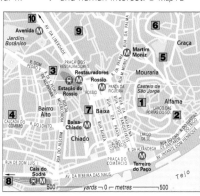

Cristo Rei was inspired by Rio de Janeiro's emblematic Christ the Saviour statue.

37

Left **Restaurant Moamba** Right **Associação Caboverdeana**

TOP 10 African Lisbon

1 Associação Caboverdeana

The Cape Verde Association has a restaurant where you can try the one-pot wonders of the islands' cuisine. It's open for lunch only, but there's live music on Tuesdays and Thursdays. *Rua Duque de Palmela 2, 8º • Map F3 • 213 531 932 • Closed Sat–Sun, D • €*

2 Poço dos Negros Area

This part of Lisbon, a short walk from the Bairro Alto, had connections with the slave trade; later it became a Little Cape Verde, where men from the islands stayed while seeking work. Most of them have now been joined by their families and moved out to the suburbs, but it still has Cape Verdean restaurants and shops. *Rua do Poço dos Negros/Rua de São Bento/Rua dos Poiais de São Bento • Map F4*

3 Casa da Morna

Part-owned by Cape Verdean musician Tito Paris, this African restaurant is more upmarket than most. It's warmly-painted, windowless but cool, and there's live music most nights. *Rua Rodrigues Faria 21 • Map D5 • 213 646 399 • Closed Sun, Mon L • €€€*

Restaurant Casa da Morna

4 São Cristovão

Cheap, chatty and cheerful, this simple Cape Verdean restaurant near the castle fills stomachs and warms hearts. *Rua de São Cristovão 28–30 • Map P3 • 218 885 578 • €*

5 Cantinho do Aziz

Aziz, from Mozambique, set up one of Lisbon's smallest and friendliest African restaurants. Now his widow and sons run his *cantinho* (corner), maintaining the feeling that you're eating in someone's frugal but welcoming home. *Rua de São Lourenço 3-5 • Map N3 • 218 876 472 • €*

Poço dos Negros

6 Enclave

Lisbon's first African disco and restaurant was opened in 1976 by Bana, a Cape Verdean singer, and still serves *cachupas* and *moambas* to the sound of live, hip-wagging music.

The disco starts at midnight, downstairs. Ⓢ Rua do Sol ao Rato 71A • Map E3 • 213 860 877 • Restaurant closed Mon–Wed; disco Fri & Sat • €€

Mussulo
An Angolan club with a well-dressed clientele dancing close together to zouk or to quicker, newer beats. Gets going late at night. Ⓢ Rua Sousa Martins 5D • Map F2 • 213 556 872 • Closed Mon & Tue

Soul Club
This big club in the nightlife area of Alcântara draws a younger crowd – mainly Angolan – dancing to Afro-techno and other music. As in most African clubs, admission is free for women; for men the charge varies. Ⓢ Travess Teixeira Júnior 6 • Map D5 • Closed Sun–Tue

Soul Club

Cantinho da Paz
Goan dishes like veal xacuti rub shoulders with African favourites like prawn moqueca (fish stew with coconut milk). Ⓢ Rua da Paz 4 • Map F4 • 213 901 963 • Closed Sun • €€

Moamba
A basic restaurant serving flavoursome dishes of various African origins. The big draw is the signature dish moamba de galinha, a chicken stew. Moamba is a short walk from some of the other African places. Ⓢ Rua Fradesso da Silveira 75 • Map D5 • 213 630 310 • Closed Sun • €€

Top 10 Ex-colonies

Angola (1648–1975)
Rich in resources, Angola was Portugal's biggest African colony until its war of liberation. Decades of civil war followed.

Mozambique (1885–1975)
Mozambique had been fighting for independence for 15 years when Portugal ceded it.

Guinea-Bissau (1446–1974)
This small west African nation declared independence unilaterally in 1973; it was recognized the following year.

Cape Verde (1456–1975)
These islands, off west Africa, were unoccupied when the Portuguese first arrived.

São Tomé & Príncipe (1522–1975)
These islands in the Gulf of Guinea became one of the world's smallest and poorest independent nations. Oil finds are now boosting the economy.

Goa (1510–1961)
Portuguese until annexed by India, it was one of the few colonies where intermarriage created a mixed community.

Timor (1511-1975)
Indonesia annexed Timor in 1975; it became independent East Timor in 2002.

Ceylon (1517–1658)
The Portuguese occupied parts of today's Sri Lanka until ousted by the Dutch.

Macau (1557-1999)
The oldest European colony in China, Macau was Portuguese-ruled for 442 years.

Brazil (1500–1822)
By far Portugal's biggest colony, taking many African slaves, Brazil became seat of the Portuguese court in 1808, then declared independence.

One meeting point for the African community in central Lisbon is outside the São Domingos church (see p32).

Left **Art-Nouveau shop, Chiado** Centre **Campo de Ourique food market** Right **Bairro Alto shoe shop**

Shopping Districts

Rua Augusta shoppers, Baixa

Baixa
The charm of the Baixa lies with its courteous shopkeepers, who still stand behind wooden counters and do sums on bits of paper. For all that, the pedestrianized Rua Augusta is lined with modern chains. ⊗ *Map M4–5*

Chiado
Traditionally the quarter with Lisbon's most elegant shops, the Chiado is now the city's most varied and rewarding shopping district. It mixes quiet streets with lively squares and sheet-music suppliers with street-cred fashion boutiques. ⊗ *Map L4*

Guerra Junqueiro/Roma
Head uptown to Avda Guerra Junqueiro and adjacent Avda Roma for good clothes shops and cafés – and a visit to *tia* territory. *Tia* means "aunt", but also signifies a

deeply tanned, jewellery-laden woman who takes her shopping seriously. ⊗ *Map G1*

Campo de Ourique/ Amoreiras
Gentrification proceeds at a genteel pace in Campo de Ourique. The grid street plan makes for lots of corner bakeries, cafés and small shops. The nearby Amoreiras Towers was Lisbon's first shopping centre. Brash and in a more trafficky location, they nevertheless provide plenty to tempt the shopper. ⊗ *Map E3*

Fresh Food Markets
Prices at Lisbon's food markets may not be lower than at supermarkets, but the produce is often fresher and the experience has an added flavour. Among the best are Mercado da Ribeira, opposite Cais do Sodré station; Mercado de Campo de Ourique, in west Lisbon; and Mercado 31 de Janeiro, behind the Saldanha Residence building on Avenida Fontes Pereira de Melo. ⊗ *Map K6, E3, F2*

Bairro Alto
Bairro Alto competes with the big shopping centres by also offering night-time shopping – in a much cooler setting, and with the possibility of sipping on a drink as you shop. Some shops here may seem ineffably trendy, but Bairro Alto is a proven nursery for Portuguese fashion and design. ⊗ *Map K3–4*

Markets open early and pack up at around lunchtime.

7 Rua de São Bento/ Rua da Escola Politécnica

Rua de São Bento is a mini-district for antiques and second-hand shops, among others. It's a short hop to pleasant Praça das Flores, for a coffee under the trees, and then an uphill walk to Rua da Escola Politécnica, where some more expensive antiques shops are clustered. ✎ Map F4

8 Santa Apolónia

Although just a row of converted warehouses, this small shopping area opposite Santa Apolónia station has some of Lisbon's most interesting shops – for music, food and design. They are spiritually presided over by the Bica do Sapato restaurant (see p44) and the adjacent Lux nightclub (see p42). ✎ Map R3

9 Feira da Ladra

Lisbon's Thieves' Market sells items like beautiful brass taps that won't fit any known plumbing. As with most flea markets, it's the sights, sounds, people and haggling that are the thing. ✎ Campo de Santa Clara • Map R2 • Tue, Sat

Feira da Ladra market

10 Avenida da Liberdade

It could be greener and wider, but Lisbon's grand avenue remains torn between its roles as road and promenade. Several international designers are not put off and have their main Lisbon shops here, alongside some venerable local merchants. ✎ Map F3

Top 10 Things to Buy

1 Ceramics
Portuguese ceramics extend beyond tiles to pottery, from the rustic to the twee.

2 Embroidery
Bordados are delicate, but lasting, old-world table linen.

3 Clothes at Markets
Rifle through fakes and failures for the odd find at Cascais on the first or third Sunday of the month, or Carcavelos on any Thursday.

4 Shoes
Fewer shoes are made in Portugal now, but those that are tend to be of higher quality.

5 Stainless Steel Cookware
There are several good-value brands of pots, pans and other kitchen essentials. Look out for Artame and Lourenço.

6 Wine
A wisely spent €5 will get you a truly good wine; €20 an unforgettable one. The wide choice is a pleasant surprise.

7 Cheese
Choose from runny Serra ewes' milk cheeses, delicious Serpa and Azeitão, peppery Castelo Branco and excellent hard and soft goats' cheeses.

8 Hams and Smoked Meats
The best presunto (cured ham) was from the north, but the Alentejan ham of the Ibérico pig is arguably better. Taste first, and decide for yourself.

9 Preserved Foods
Sardines and other tinned fish, olives, olive oil, massa de pimentão (red-pepper paste) and chilli sauces are all superb.

10 Beauty Treatments
Lisbon's beauty salons are labour-intensive rather than high-tech and offer good value.

One-stop shopping until late at night is available at Lisbon's many shopping malls, including Colombo and Vasco da Gama.

Left **Lux** Right **Alcântara-Mar**

🔟 Bars and Nightclubs

1 Lux
Lux is Lisbon's most stylish and varied nightclub. With a downstairs dance floor, an upstairs bar and dance area, a roof-top terrace, groovy retro decor and a string of hot DJs, there is substance to the hype. ⌾ Cais da Pedra, Avenida Infante Dom Henrique • Map R3

2 Alcântara-Mar
Revered in the 1990s, the Alcântara-Mar is still kicking up a dancing frenzy with techno music and a mixed crowd.
⌾ Rua da Cozinha Economica 11 • Map D5

3 Paradise Garage
One of Lisbon's best-known live venues, Paradise Garage reopened in late 2010 with more of a club music concept and occasional live concerts. ⌾ Rua João Oliveira Miguéis 38–48 • Map D5

4 Belém Bar Café
Set in a prime riverside location in the tourist centre of Belém, BBC is a one-stop shop for clubbing and fine dining with Lisbon's trendiest crowd. Open Tuesday to Saturday, it features the hottest dance floor hits. In the summer there are outdoor bar and dance floor areas with fine views of the Tagus. ⌾ Avenida de Brasilia, Pavilhão Poente • Map C6

5 Bar Lounge
Owner and resident disc-spinner Mário Valente has been working to enrich Bar Lounge's eclectic mix of indie and electronic pop and rock since the early noughties. Located down an alley, its full programme of live bands, combined with a relaxed atmosphere, have earned it a loyal following. ⌾ Rua da Moeda 1 • Map J5

6 Kremlin
Kremlin was the first big dance club in Lisbon and it is still a great place to go if you really want to get down and dance the night away. There is just a whiff of danger about the place; the door-men always seem to be on edge. ⌾ Escadinhas da Praia 5 • Map E5

7 Incógnito
This veteran of the early 1990s has kept on doing what it does best and draws a mostly low-profile crowd. Sized between a bar and a club, it accommodates both

Belém Bar Café

➡ Bairro Alto has Lisbon's greatest concentration of small bars (see p76) chilling and grooving. The music is a mixed bag, with recent dance sounds on week nights and a broader spectrum at weekends. Ⓢ *Rua dos Poiais de São Bento 37* • *Map F4*

Bar do Rio
What is arguably Lisbon's grooviest club occupies certainly the most successful warehouse conversion along the quays. The space isn't huge, the crowd is far from pimply, and the atmosphere is slightly glamorous yet relaxed, enhanced by mellow house and funky sounds. Ⓢ *Armazém A, Porta 7, Cais do Sodré* • *Map K6*

Op Art

Op Art
A beacon of taste and good music in the Docas area, Op Art is a small glass pavilion by the river, used as a café-restaurant during the day and a discerning DJ bar throughout the night. Late evenings and dawns can be magical. Ⓢ *Doca de Santo Amaro* • *Map D6*

Jamaica
In a fading red-light district and much beloved among seekers of old Lisbon, Jamaica caters broadly to nostalgia and the need to dance. The crowd is mixed – hip young things and greying types who can't work out the current musical vibe – and the mood easy. Tuesday nights are dedicated to reggae; others offer a cocktail of styles. Ⓢ *Rua Nova de Carvalho 6–8* • *Map K6*

Fado Venues

Clube de Fado
This essential Alfama *fado* venue is owned by *guitarrista* Mário Pacheco, who showcases new stars. Ⓢ *Rua de São João da Praça 94* • *218 852 704*

Parreirinha de Alfama
A traditional venue owned by the famous Argentina Santos. Ⓢ *Beco do Espírito Santo 1* • *218 868 209*

Senhor Vinho
Quality and style, rather than grit, characterize the singing at this expensive *fado* restaurant. Ⓢ *Rua do Meio à Lapa 18* • *213 972 681*

Timpanas
Timpanas offers a superb dinner show with first-class *fado*. Ⓢ *Rua Gilberto Rola 24* • *213 906 655*

Tasca do Chico
Gritty *fado vadio*: amateur impromptu performances. Ⓢ *Rua dos Remédios 83* • *965 059 670*

Café Luso
Offering first-class *fado* and fine food in the heart of the Bairro Alto since the 1920s. Ⓢ *Travessa da Queimada 10* • *213 422 281*

Os Ferreiras
A small grill restaurant and a serious *fado* venue. Ⓢ *Rua de São Lázaro 150* • *218 850 851*

A Severa
Named after the famous 19th-century gypsy *fadista*. Ⓢ *Rua das Gáveas 51* • *218 428 314*

Casa de Linhares
The *fado* side of a *bacalhau* restaurant. Ⓢ *Beco dos Armazéns do Linho 2* • *218 865 088*

O Faia
One of Bairro Alto's larger *fado* venues. Good music, expensive food. Ⓢ *Rua da Barroca 54* • *213 426 742*

Fado (literally "Fate") is Lisbon's own music, with a tradition going back over 150 years. Museu do Fado (see p58) is a good place to start.

Left **Bica do Sapato** Right **A Travessa**

🔟 Restaurants

1 Eleven
A Modernist window box at the top of Parque Eduardo VII is the setting for Lisbon's most sophisticated contemporary restaurant. Joachim Koerper and his team have already bagged a Michelin star for the meticulously prepared food; he is aiming for a second. ✎ *Rua Marquês da Fronteira, Jardim Amália Rodrigues • Map E2 • 213 862 211 • Closed Sun • €€€€€*

2 Bica do Sapato
Size and experience keep Bica do Sapato ahead of newer contemporary restaurants in Lisbon. Downstairs there is a bar and a dining room; upstairs a sushi restaurant. Fish is the thing here – but not the usual grilled versions served with potatoes. ✎ *Avenida Infante Dom Henrique/Cais da Pedra, Armazém B • Map R3 • 218 810 320 • Closed Sun & Mon L • €€€€*

3 Espaço Lisboa
With a stylish interior, Espaço Lisboa is just a stone's throw from the main cruise terminal. Serving traditional Portuguese cuisine, there's a good choice of fish options and classic meat dishes such as veal

Eleven

in port wine. Upstairs there's live jazz on Friday nights and a 1970s and '80s disco on Saturdays. ✎ *Rua da Cozinha Económica 16 • Map D5 • 213 610 210 • Closed L • €€€*

4 Real Fábrica
Justa and António Nobre already have their place in the annals of Portuguese gastronomy assured for their Nobre restaurant in Ajuda. At this first-floor place near Largo do Rato, you can try Justa's crab soup, served in the shell, or her dishes based on pheasant or grouper. ✎ *Rua da Escola Politécnica 275 • Map F3 • 213 852 090 • Closed Sun • €€€€*

5 A Travessa
In the grand surroundings of an old convent (shared with a puppet museum and private residents) is this welcoming restaurant that feels like it could be in a provincial town. The food, though, is cosmopolitan, successfully mixing Portuguese, Belgian and French influences to gourmet effect. ✎ *Travessa do Convento das Bernardas 12 • Map F5 • 213 902 034 • Closed Sat L, Sun & Mon L • €€€€*

6 Casa do Alentejo
Overlooking a wonderful Moorish-style interior courtyard, this "embassy of the Alentejo region" is one of Lisbon's most memorable dining locations. Stick to soups, rice dishes or fish and you won't forget the food either. ✎ *Rua das Portas de Santo Antão 58 (upstairs) • Map L2 • 213 405 140 • €€*

Tavares

A cavern of gilt, stucco, and heavy mirrors, Tavares, opened in 1784, claims to be Lisbon's oldest restaurant; the impressive decor, though, is early 20th-century. The fortunes of this restaurant have fluctuated, but with a French chef at the helm, it appears as enduring as ever.
◈ Rua da Misericórdia 37 • Map L4 • 213 421 112 • Closed Sun & Mon • €€€€€

Tavares

Laurentina

The self-proclaimed "King of Cod", this popular eatery offers an exhaustive range of bacalhau.
◈ Avenida Conde de Valbom 71A • Map F1 • 217 960 260 • Closed Sun • €€€

La Moneda

Modern food in a modern setting was La Moneda's aim. Prices have risen, along with culinary ambitions, but the informality makes it great for a social meal.
◈ Rua da Moeda 1C • Map J5 • 213 908 012 • Closed Sun • €€€

Manifesto

Funky Pop Art graphics decorate the walls, while the kitchen produces some truly inspiring tasting menus. Pan-fried beef tenderloin with red bell-pepper fricassee is typical. ◈ Largo de Santos 9C • Map F5 • 213 963 419 • Closed Sat L, Sun & Mon • €€€€€

Top 10 Cafés and *Pastelarias*

1 Antiga Confeitaria de Belém
The birthplace of the original *pastel de nata* is a site of pilgrimage (see p86).

2 Confeitaria Nacional
Here you will spot many rotund ladies bearing cardboard boxes tied with string – a sure sign of quality (see p68).

3 Bénard
For cakes, this is a better option than the crowded A Brasileira next door (see p75).

4 Casa Suiça
Classy but affordable café with outdoor tables on both Rossio and Praça da Figueira (see p68).

5 Leitaria Caneças
This quality bakery and pastry shop near the British Bar (see p68) is also a café.
◈ Rua Bernardino Costa 36

6 Café Mexicana
A classic Lisbon café-restaurant and social club – big and busy (see p95).

7 Pastelaria Versailles
Dream your way back to a time before fast food in this unreformed relic of old Lisbon (see p95).

8 Panificação Mecânica
Its name taken from its early use of baking machinery, this bakery and pastry shop is an Art-Nouveau jewel.
◈ Rua Silva Carvalho 209–25

9 Pau de Canela
This café has a terrace on the small but sweet Praça das Flores. Children can play safely nearby. ◈ Praça das Flores 27

10 O Chá da Lapa
Experience a Lisbon tea salon – for the cakes, the atmosphere and the smart Lapa ladies. ◈ Rua do Olival 8–10

For more restaurant listings, and a guide to restaurant price bands See pp61, 69, 77, 85, 89, 95 and 103

Left **Buying fish at Rua de São Pedro fish market** Right **Pastéis de Nata**

🔟 Culinary Highlights

1 Arroz de Marisco

This king of Portuguese rice dishes is more moist than a paella and less sticky than a risotto. It should contain shellfish, in the shell for flavour (lobster claws, pieces of spider crab, prawns, clams and cockles), as well as a streak of chilli and a liberal sprinkling of fresh coriander. Many restaurants cook it once a week and serve it in enormous portions.

2 Açorda

Originally a poor man's soup from the Alentejo, Açorda was simply water flavoured with garlic and oil, and thickened with a slice of yesterday's bread and an egg. Most restaurants now do a more sophisticated version in which the soup is a sort of purée, studded with seafood *(marisco)* or served with small fillets of deep-fried fish. Pap'Açorda *(see p77)* makes one of the best.

Açorda de Marisco

3 Bacalhau

Foreign visitors may find it strange that the Portuguese have such a passion for salted dried cod, fished in distant seas, when they have such a delectable fresh selection much closer at hand. The explanation involves history, economics, Salazar *(see p31)* and habit. Small croquettes of

bacalhau and mashed potatoes, *pastéis de bacalhau*, are a good introduction; then you are ready to sample some of the remaining 364 ways of preparing *bacalhau*.

4 Frango à Piri-piri

Many a visitor's fondest food memory of Portugal, this is simply grilled chicken served with chilli oil *(piri-piri* is the Portuguese-African term for chilli). The simplicity is deceptive, though: in the best versions of the dish, the chicken has been treated to a thorough marinade before grilling.

5 Ameijoas à Bulhão Pato

All truly great dishes combine just a few flavours, with a minimum of fuss. This one is a prime example: *ameijoa* clams cooked briefly in their own juices, olive oil and plenty of whole, crushed garlic cloves, and served with coriander and lemon wedges. Bread is the only accompaniment.

6 Fresh Fish

Go to a good fishmonger and you will be presented with an encyclopedic choice of fish, from bass and bream to John Dory, eel, skate and parrot fish. Good restaurants for sampling some of these include Bica do Sapato *(see p44)* and Porto de Santa Maria *(see p103)*.

7 Smoked and Cured Ham and Meats

Presunto is the Portuguese name for cured ham. Usually dried in salt, it is sometimes also smoked, and often rolled in bright orange paprika powder. *Enchidos* is the collective term for a bewildering but rewarding array of sausages and salamis. These are often heavily smoked and spiced.

8 Pastéis de Nata

Small custard tarts are a staple of Lisbon cafés, taken on the run with a piercing *bica*, the city's term for espresso. Sometimes sprinkled with cinnamon and always reassuringly gooey, they are made to the original recipe at the Antiga Confeitaria in Belém *(see p86)*. All others are imitations, so they say.

9 Soups

Soup in Portugal is the traditional meal opener, and is often made with vegetables (though the stock will almost invariably be chicken, with bits of smoked sausage, *chouriço*, added as spice). The most famous is *caldo verde*, made with the kale that grows in the north – shredded in a special machine – and potato, and spiced with *chouriço*. One of the richest is *sopa da pedra* (stone soup), containing a little bit of everything (and a stone, according to the legend).

10 Picanha

Picanha was originally a Brazilian cut of rump steak, grilled whole and served in thin slices with black-bean stew and other accompaniments. However, it has become so popular that it is now made with local cuts of beef and served in many non-Brazilian restaurants. It is very flavourful, if not always tender meat.

Top 10 Portuguese Wines

1 Quinta do Vale Meão
One of the best modern reds is made with grapes from the vineyards far up the Douro valley that used to supply the legendary Barca Velha.

2 Niepoort
Originally Dutch, this family-owned port shipper has emerged as one of the great innovators in table wines.

3 Quinta do Crasto
This is a quality producer of modern Douro wine and good-value port, particularly the unfiltered LBVs.

4 Ferreira
A Douro institution, home of Barca Velha and of later greats such as Quinta da Leda.

5 Vallado
A reliable producer of Douro reds in the muscular category, Vallado is superb value and a Douro vanguard.

6 Quinta da Pellada
One of the best Dão producers of the day makes wines that are more elegant than many from the Douro.

7 Quinta do Monte d'Oiro
This Estremadura producer shows the region is capable of great wines – made mainly from French grapes.

8 Tapada de Coelheiros
Some of the region's most concentrated reds come from this small Alentejo wine maker.

9 Esporão
One of the success stories of the Alentejo makes reds and whites, varietals and blends, of reliably high quality.

10 João Portugal Ramos
This company is purveyor of some of the most popular modern Portuguese wines.

Left **Sandy beach and promenade along the bay of Estoril** Right **Guincho beach**

🔟 Beaches

1 Caparica North
The northern stretch of the Caparica coast is the busiest, with Caparica town, plus mid-range hotels, holiday homes, camp sites and restaurants.

2 Caparica Centre
Heading south, the beach gets less busy, but has fewer amenities. From late spring to early autumn the Transpraia train runs from Caparica town to Fonte da Telha, stopping at bars and restaurants en route. The beach at Fonte da Telha is busy and family-oriented. Many bars are closed out of season.

Caparica Centre

3 Carcavelos
The broadest and longest beach along the Estoril coast is far enough from Lisbon for clean water and yet close enough for an afternoon outing. Though its reputation suffered after a single, much-publicized "robbery stampede" in 2005, in which groups of youths on the beach

Carcavelos

suddenly grabbed valuables from their neighbours, security has as a result been stepped up. Carcavelos is still extremely pleasant out of season.

4 Lagoa de Albufeira and Meco
The southern half of the Caparica coast is accessible only by driving towards Sesimbra – or after a very long walk along the beach. Lagoa de Albufeira, a lagoon, is popular for wind-surfing. Meco, further south, is backed by a village with restaurants and bars.

5 Estoril and Cascais
These beaches get crowded as they are mostly short and narrow. Still, the promenade that runs just above them, all the way from Estoril to Cascais, is full of relaxed bars and eateries, where you can also take the sun.

6 Guincho
Guincho can provide an eyeful of sand on a windy day, but experienced surfers love it and it gives the fullest taste of nature of all the beaches along the Estoril coast. Beyond the built-up outskirts of Cascais, and with the Sintra hills as a backdrop, it is a beautiful spot with magnificent beaches and draws the crowds on summer weekends. To avoid parking

hassles, rent a bicycle in Cascais and ride out on the track that runs alongside the spectacular coast road.

Ursa

Not marked on maps and requiring a steep descent along narrow paths, Ursa is one of the most secluded beaches in the region. Surrounded by towering cliffs like giants seated in the surf, there are no amenities and anything beyond a short swim near the beach is ill advised. The beach is reached along the road to Cabo da Roca, where there is a small sign marked Ursa. Park your car out of sight of the main road (don't leave any valuables in it) and head down the path.

Adraga

Adraga

Beyond Cabo da Roca, this pretty beach is reached via Almoçageme, off the Sintra road. The area is affected by Sintra's cooler climate. The single restaurant is excellent.

Grande

With the longest unbroken stretch of sand in the area, Grande is popular with surfers and body boarders. There are bars and restaurants, and one hotel.

Das Maçãs

"Apple Beach" is one of the most family-friendly along the Sintra-Colares coast. Lots of good seafood restaurants are to be found nearby.

Top 10 Outdoor Activities

Walking
For dirt rather than cobbles underfoot, head for Sintra, Arrábida or the Tejo estuary.

Cycling
Though rare in Lisbon, bikes can be rented in Cascais and Parque das Nações.

Board Sports
Surfing and body-boarding are big along the Estoril and Sintra coasts, as is kite surfing on the Caparica coast.

Fishing
Fishermen seem to be all along the river and beaches. There are good spots near Cascais, where boats are used.

Bird-watching
The Tagus marshlands beyond Alcochete and the Tróia peninsula are rich in bird life at almost all times of year.

Sailing
There are sailing schools in Parque das Nações, Belém and along the Estoril coast. Renting larger craft is possible.

Horse Riding
There are a number of *equestre* or *hípico* clubs around Cascais and Sintra, and at Belas nearer Lisbon.

Jogging
The western river front is reasonable jogging territory, as is Parque Eduardo VII. Monsanto and the Guincho coast are other options.

Mountain Biking
Lisbon hosts a small but hotly contested downhill bike race each May, the Lisbon Downtown. For country tracks, head to Sintra or Arrábida.

Roller Skating
Parque das Nações, the Alcântara docks and Belém all have areas suited to skating.

Surf forecasts for Portugal can be found on www.surf-forecast.com

Left **Oceanário** Right **Monsanto**

🔟 Activities for Children

1 Monsanto
"Lisbon's lungs" is an unruly pine wood on the city's western fringes. The Parque Recreativo do Alto da Serafina and Parque Infantil do Alvito are fenced-off, well-equipped play parks (see p83). ⊗ Map D2

2 Jardim Zoológico
Lisbon's zoo has features that are particularly popular with children. These include a train and an open-air cable car, which allows you to view many of the enclosures from above. Other attractions include an aquatic show with dolphins and sea lions, and a good reptile house.
⊗ Praça Marechal Humberto Delgado • Map D1 • Mar–Sep: 10am–8pm daily; Oct–Feb: 10am–6pm daily (last adm 1 hr 15 mins before closing) • Adm charge

Sea Lion at Lisbon Zoo

3 Oceanário
Opened for the 1998 Lisbon Expo, the Oceanarium remains the biggest single attraction in Parque das Nações. The second-

Knowledge Pavilion – Ciência Viva

largest aquarium in the world, it holds an impressive array of species (see pp16–17).

4 Knowledge Pavilion – Ciência Viva
This hands-on science museum has vast halls full of intriguing gadgetry to illustrate important fundamental laws of nature as well as more exotic phenomena. Downstairs, the youngest visitors get the chance to don hard hats and help build the Unfinished House (see pp16–17).

5 Quinta Pedagógica
This city farm gives children the chance to handle baby animals and learn about rural activities and crafts. ⊗ Rua Cidade de Lobito • Map C1 • May–Sep: 9am–7pm Tue–Fri, 10am–7pm Sat & Sun; Oct–Apr: 9am–5:30pm Tue–Fri, 10am–5:30pm Sat & Sun

6 Colombo
Lisbon's mega-mall has a Funcenter on the top floor, with slot machines, games and rides, plus a bowling alley. ⊗ Avenida Lusíada • Map B2 • Noon–midnight Mon–Fri, 11am–midnight Sat & Sun

7 Roller Skating, Ice Skating and Skateboarding
There are several places in Lisbon with ramps and rinks for feet with wheels. Two of the best are on Avenida Brasília by the Alcântara

Quinta Pedagógica

Docks, and by the Vasco da Gama tower in Parque das Nações. In winter, there is an outdoor ice rink near Largo de Santos.

Swimming Pools
Many hotels have outdoor pools, but for those without, the Clube Nacional de Natação has a complex at Rua de São Bento 209, with indoor and outdoor pools. An alternative is Olaias Clube at Rua Robalo Gouveia in east Lisbon.

Beaches
Beaches are great places for children, but the Atlantic is not the safest water for young ones to play in. Low tide is a good time for building sand castles and wallowing in pools left by the receding sea. Some of the beaches along the Estoril coast (see p48) are more protected; otherwise head for Portinho de Arrábida or Tróia (see p52).

Museu de Ciência
Housed in the grand setting of the old Polytechnic, this science museum by the Jardim Botânico (see p80) has an ageing but engaging hands-on exhibit illustrating basic principles of physics. ⑤ Rua da Escola Politécnica 58 • Map J2 • Open 10am–5pm Tue–Fri, 11am–6pm Sat & Sun • Adm charge

Top 10 Family-friendly Restaurants

1 Casanova
A popular quay-side pizzeria with a safe veranda; kids can even watch the chef (see p61).

2 31 da Armada
Plus points at this place include the traffic-free square and friendly staff. ⑤ Praça da Armada 31 • 213 976 330

3 Nosolo Itália
Pizzas, pastas and ice creams are served on a large outdoor terrace (see p85).

4 Café Buenos Aires
The steps outside are traffic free; inside, the vibe is accommodating (see p77).

5 Psi
The location, in a garden with ponds, adds to parents' relaxation; the no-alcohol policy may not (see p95).

6 Papagaio da Serafina
A pavilion-style restaurant with an ambitious menu in Monsanto's best children's park. ⑤ Parque Recreativo do Alto da Serafina • 217 742 888

7 Jardim dos Sentidos
Here vegetarian food is served in a lovely space with an interior garden. ⑤ Rua da Mãe d'Água 3 • 213 423 670

8 Restaurants at Doca de Santo Amaro
Facing a marina, these eateries have outdoor tables and attract families. ⑤ Doca de Santo Amaro

9 Restaurants in Parque das Nações
Choices range from food courts to riverside terraces; steak houses to floating restaurants. ⑤ Parque das Nações

10 Restaurants along Rua Vieira Portuense
This short street of outdoor restaurants in Belém overlooks the Jardim de Belém (see p85).

Lisbon's Top 10

 Original-language screenings of children's films are listed as v.o., for versão original.

Left **Crenellated Óbidos** Right **Spring flowers by the saltpans of the Tejo estuary near Alcochete**

🔟 Excursions

1 Sintra hills
The romantic beauty of Sintra *(see pp26–7)* and its palaces, the crumbling walls veiled with moss, the views, the winding roads under dense canopies of leaves, the smell of the air and the thoughts evoked make Sintra and its hills a magical world.

2 Serra da Arrábida
This limestone massif, about 40 minutes south of Lisbon by car, provides in its vegetation and calm, blue-green waters Portugal's most Mediterranean scenery. It also has dramatic cliffs. Head for Portinho da Arrábida, and stop often as you get close.

3 Palmela and Azeitão
The main sight in Palmela is the hill-top castle, now an elegant *pousada* open to passing visitors. Vila Fresca de Azeitão and Vila Nogueira de Azeitão are neigh-bouring towns at the heart of the Palmela wine country.

Aerial view of Palmela's castle

4 Setúbal and Tróia
The port town of Setúbal is prosaic, but it is home to the Igreja de Jesus, the first and perhaps most distinctive example of the Manueline style. People and cars are ferried across the mouth of the Sado river to the finger-like peninsula of Tróia, with excellent, undeveloped beaches extending south and a rich bird life on its estuary side.

5 Alcácer do Sal
The name itself is a bilingual history lesson, mixing the Arabic for castle and the Portuguese for salt. The town's once-Moorish castle is now a *pousada*, while the salt trade that dates back two millennia now plays a smaller role than rice-growing.

6 Tejo Estuary
The Tejo estuary is easily accessible from Lisbon via the town of Alcochete, just across the Vasco da Gama bridge. From here you can venture into the *lezíria* marshlands by car or on foot. This area is one of Europe's ten most important staging sites for migrating water birds, including flamingo, black-tailed godwit and avocet.

7 Mafra
Mafra is home to an extra-vagant palace and monastery built for Dom João V, Portugal's 18th-century monarch with a weakness for excesses of all kinds. The almost pyramidal

Driving in Portugal requires composure and vigilance. Ignore provocations by other drivers.

Library at Mafra's palace

proportions of its construction are entertainingly detailed in José Saramago's novel *Balthazar and Blimunda*. The hunting grounds are now used for a wolf conservation project.

Óbidos
Óbidos is arguably the most picturesque town in Portugal, contained within the walls of a 14th-century castle and filled with whitewashed houses whose edges are painted ochre or blue and whose windows wear lace curtains and geraniums in pots. The town was the wedding gift of Dom Dinis to his queen, Isabel of Aragon, in 1282.

Vila Franca de Xira
A centre for bullfighting, this town hosts the *Festa do Colete Encarnado* in July every year, a raucous and showy festival that includes bull-running. A similar festival, the *Feira do Outubro*, is held in October.

Ribatejo Wine Route
Some of the best wine producers in the Ribatejo region are clustered on the left bank of the Tejo, just north of Vila Franca de Xira, particularly between the towns of Almeirim and Alpiarça. Most welcome visitors. Seek out Quinta do Casal Branco, Quinta da Alorna, Fiuza & Bright and Quinta da Lagoalva de Cima.

Top 10 Beauty Spots

1 Guincho Coast
Cars drive very slowly – a rare thing in Portugal – along this scenic coast road, to take in the natural beauty.

2 Castelo dos Mouros
The steeply stepped walls of this attractive old castle offer fabulous views.

3 Penedo
This village on the high road from Sintra to the coast is misty and romantic in winter and a cool refuge in summer.

4 Peninha
A vantage point for views of Europe's western edge and a small group of buildings with an intriguing history *(see p102)*.

5 Ursa
This beach is worth visiting out of season, and without swimming gear, for the sheer beauty of the place *(see p49)*.

6 Monserrate
The gardens and palace-pavilion of Monserrate, with a history of English gardeners and visitors, remain popular.

7 Portinho da Arrábida
One of the most protected beaches along the entire western seaboard looks as if it belongs in Croatia or Turkey.

8 Pancas and Around
If you prefer flat expanses with huge skies and endless views, head for this hamlet just northeast of Alcochete, on the edge of the *lezíria*.

9 Cabo Espichel
The cliff-top southwestern-most point of the Setúbal peninsula is in some ways more attractive than the more illustrious Cabo da Roca.

10 Bucelas and Beyond
Head here for a taste of rolling inland Estremadura – and some great white wine.

AROUND
LISBON

Alfama, Castelo
& the East
56–61

Baixa to Restauradores
62–69

Chiado & Bairro Alto
70–77

West Lisbon
80–89

Avenida
& North Lisbon
90–95

Lisbon Coast
98–103

LISBON'S TOP 10

Left **Museu do Teatro Romano** Right **Largo das Portas do Sol**

Alfama, Castelo & the East

ALFAMA'S ARABIC-SOUNDING NAME AND ANTHILL LAYOUT *are testament to its past as an important district of Moorish Lisbon – or, more likely, originally two districts: one on the riverside of fishermen and sea folk, and one on the hillside of higher society. No buildings survive from this era, but Alfama suffered little damage in the 1755 earthquake, so its medieval street plan has remained intact. And that is what makes it such a joy to explore, without the interference of traffic. The Castelo neighbourhood at the top adjoins the higher hill district of Graça and also Mouraria, a less touristic area. To the south and east, Alfama descends to the river.*

Castelo de São Jorge

Sights

1. Castelo de São Jorge
2. Museu do Teatro Romano
3. Sé Catedral
4. Largo das Portas do Sol
5. Largo de São Miguel
6. Museu do Fado
7. Santo Estevão
8. Igreja de Santa Engrácia/ Panteão Nacional
9. Fundação Ricardo do Espírito Santo Silva
10. Museu Nacional do Azulejo

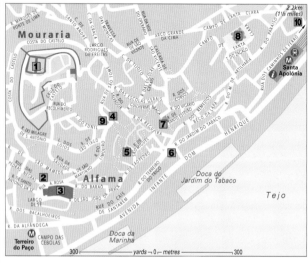

Preceding pages **Spiral staircase descending into initiation well, Quinta da Regaleira, Sintra**

Castelo de São Jorge
The castle that crowns Alfama was the heart of the city in the Moorish era, and the site goes back to Phoenician times at least. The picturesque residential area within the castle's outer walls is also called Castelo (see pp8–9).

Museu do Teatro Romano
A Roman amphitheatre from the 1st century BC lurks beneath the buildings just above the Sé. Not a lot has yet been excavated, but it seems to have been large, seating maybe 5,000. Excavations continue, so visitors get an insight into archeological work.
Ⓢ Pátio do Aljube 5 • Map N4 • 218 820 320 • Open 10am–1pm, 2–6pm Tue–Sun

Sé Catedral
The English crusader Gilbert of Hastings, Lisbon's first bishop, oversaw the construction of the city's cathedral in the mid-12th century. The site was previously occupied by a mosque, parts of which have been excavated in the cloister (see pp12–13).

Largo das Portas do Sol
When the 28 tram gets to the top of the hill beyond the Sé, it squeezes between two buildings

A street in the area of Saõ Miguel

in what used to be the Moorish-era city walls. From here there is one of the best views of Alfama and the river. Backtrack past the Santa Luzia church, where the tram squeezed by, and you reach the Miradouro de Santa Luzia, one of the city's official viewpoints (see p36). Across the street are two access routes to the castle. There are several outdoor cafés in the area. Ⓢ Map P4

Largo de São Miguel
You can reach this square in the heart of Alfama via steps from Largo das Portas do Sol: walk down next to Santa Luzia church and bear left after the first corner. This is the essence of Alfama: narrow alleys that white-haired residents use as gardens, grills the size of shoe-boxes with sardines smoking, patios, archways and twisting stairs. The blissful absence of cars lets children play everywhere. Largo de São Miguel is at the centre of the huge party thrown to honour St Anthony, Lisbon's principal patron saint on 12 June every year. Ⓢ Map P4

Sé Catedral

Museu do Fado

6 Also called the Casa do Fado e da Guitarra Portuguesa, this is dedicated to Lisbon's most famous musical genre and to the mandolin-shaped Portuguese "guitar". The instrument, whose strings are in pairs, combines with the singer's soaring tremolos to give Fado – often compared with the Blues – its unique sound. The museum is surprisingly recent, but its life-size replica of a Fado venue – complete with models of singer, musicians, staff and customers – has an old-fashioned feeling to it. There is an outdoor café, and concerts are held from time to time.

⊗ Largo do Chafariz de Dentro 1
• 218 823 470 • 10am–6pm Tue–Sun
• Adm charge

Santo Estevão

7 The small esplanade in front of the Santo Estevão church is one of the area's best viewing

Marble interior, Igreja de Santa Engrácia

points. Access is easy, if steep, from Largo do Chafariz do Dentro, at the foot of Alfama, where you will find one of the city's oldest public fountains (as well as the Fado Museum, so you can easily combine a visit to both). Just head up Rua dos Remédios until you see steps on your left called Escadas de Santo Estevão; climb them and you're there. ⊗ Map Q4

Igreja de Santa Engrácia/ Panteão Nacional

8 The soaring dome of Santa Engrácia is a landmark on Lisbon's low eastern skyline, but when you approach it on foot it seems to duck out of view at every turn. This serves to remind you that the dome was added as recently as 1966, 284 years after the construction of the church began. This in turn has enriched the Portuguese language with a saying that translates as "a job like Santa Engrácia", for any interminable project. Built on a Greek cross plan with rounded arms, the church has similarities to St Peter's Basilica in Rome,

---

Saint Anthony of the Sardines

The celebration of St Anthony, on 12 June, falls close to the feast-days of other saints (São João and São Pedro, or John and Peter) and has been turned into a two-week party known as the *Festas dos Santos Populares*. In fact, the city has gone one up on this and declared the whole month *Festas da Cidade*, with a full programme of events. Concerts, shows, processions and ceremonies aside, the real party is in Largo de São Miguel in Alfama, on the night of 12 June. Tables are set up everywhere, grills are fired up and loaded with sardines covered in coarse salt, the wine and beer flow freely, bands play, children run riot, lovers woo and grannies gossip. For a taste of sardines in the right setting, and of good-natured Lisbon neighbourliness, there's no better occasion.

---

although Santa Engrácia is even-sided. The airy, marble-clad interior serves as the National Pantheon (see p32).

9 Fundação Ricardo do Espírito Santo Silva

Named after the banker who bequeathed a 17th-century Alfama palace filled with his collections of decorative arts, this foundation's museum displays an extensive collection of Portuguese, French and English furniture in period settings. Next door are workshops for traditional crafts such as cabinet-making, gilding and bookbinding. The foundation also runs two schools of arts and crafts, in other locations. ⊗ Largo das Portas do Sol 2 • Map P4 • 218 881 991 • 10am–5pm Wed–Mon • Adm charge

10 Museu Nacional do Azulejo

Beyond Alfama, in the eastern Xabregas district, is the Tile Museum, housed in a stunning former 16th-century convent with an elaborately decorated church. Highlights include a small Manueline cloister, a 23-m (75-ft) panel of painted tiles showing Lisbon in the 1740s, and extensive collections of Moorish and Portuguese tiles. The café-restaurant is a pleasant place to take a break (see pp20–21).

Museu Nacional do Azulejo

Alfama Wandering

Morning

Alfama is really the sort of place to wander around with an open mind rather than an open book. Like most labyrinthine medieval quarters it is actually quite small, but it seems large to the first-time visitor. Here are a few pointers, to get you on your way to losing your way. The street that begins on the right side of the Sé, briefly called **Cruzes da Sé** and then **Rua de São João da Praça**, is a good point of entry. There are also some worthwhile cafés and bars along here, including **Pois** and **Ondajazz** Bar (see p60). Don't turn right off this street, or you'll be led down and out of the maze. Instead, keep going and follow it round, and you'll eventually reach **Rua de São Pedro**, which leads down to **Largo do Chafariz do Dentro**, where there's a good choice of restaurants for lunch.

Afternoon

To return to the maze, head back up Rua de São Pedro and do a near 180-degree turn at the top to reach **Igreja de São Miguel**. Now you are into beco (alley) territory. Follow left turns by right turns and you should be able to weave your way to **Santo Estevão**. Should thirst overcome you, head down the steps to **PÁTIO 13**. A brisk walk up Rua dos Remedios and then along Rua do Paraíso will get you to **Campo de Santa Clara** and, if it's Tuesday or Saturday, the **Feira da Ladra** (see p41). If it's not, stroll down to the riverside row of converted warehouses at **Santa Apolónia** for another kind of shopping experience (see pp60–61).

Left **Chapitô** Right **Pois, Café**

TOP 10 Bars and Cafés

1 Cerca Moura
Right by the Portas do Sol viewpoint is this popular, largely outdoor bar and café. Indoors, it's a cosy cubbyhole inside what was once Moorish Lisbon's town walls. ⓢ *Largo das Portas do Sol 4 • Map P4*

2 Bar das Imagens
The outdoor tables have a great view at sunset but stand on a slight incline; people have been known to slide off their chairs before they've finished their first drink. The restaurant inside is strong on starters. ⓢ *Calçada Marquês de Tancos 1 • Map N4*

3 Chapitô
This large, friendly bar, café and restaurant offers a variety of seating areas and superb views. The complex is owned by a school of performing arts. ⓢ *Costa do Castelo 7 • Map N4*

4 Santiago Alquimista
Set in the spacious basement of a drama school, this bar is at the vanguard of Lisbon's musical and multicultural scene. ⓢ *Rua de Santiago 19 • Map P4*

5 Pois, Café
This living-room-style café, with a cool but relaxed vibe, was a first in Lisbon when it was opened by its Austrian owners. *Pois* is a much-used Portuguese word that evidently sounded quaint to Austrian ears. ⓢ *Rua de São João da Praça 93–5 • Map P5*

6 Ondajazz Bar
The French team behind this pleasant bar lays on live jazz and other cool musical choices in this vaulted former coffee warehouse. ⓢ *Arco de Jesus 7 • Map P5*

7 Esplanada da Igreja da Graça
One of Lisbon's best café-table views is to be had from the esplanade by the vast Graça church *(see p33)*. Particularly good on sunny late afternoons, it is less attractive after sunset. ⓢ *Largo da Graça • Map P2*

8 Deli Delux
This is a well-stocked deli with a café at the back and a small terrace. Its weekend brunches are great, but come early to avoid having to wait for a table – though there are plenty of shops to distract you if you do. ⓢ *Avenida Infante Dom Henrique/Cais da Pedra, Armazém B, Loja 8 • Map R3*

9 Wine Bar do Castelo
More than 150 Portuguese wines can be tasted here, along with a selection of meats and cheeses. A refreshing oasis right next to the castle. ⓢ *Rua Bartolomeu de Gusmão 13 • Map N4*

10 Última Sé
This DJ-driven bar in a narrow alley behind the Sé *(see pp12–13)* has a tiny dance floor, themed party nights and occasional live acts. ⓢ *Travessa do Almargem 1 • Map N5*

Around Town – Alfama, Castelo & the East

 Check the Agenda Cultural (see p107) for events listings at some of the bars above.

Casa do Leão

Price Categories

For a three course meal for one with half a bottle of wine (or equivalent meal), taxes and extra charges.	€ under €15
	€€ €15–€20
	€€€ €20–€30
	€€€€ €30–€40
	€€€€€ over €40

🔟 Restaurants

1 Bica do Sapato
Lisbon's most talked-about restaurant is an airy 1970s-retro space by the river, with modern food and a sushi bar upstairs. Trendy but not tediously so, it is part owned by John Malkovich (see p44).

2 Casanova
Lisbon's best pizzas are served at this lively restaurant with a terrace on the quay. No bookings are taken, so arrive early to avoid a wait. ⊗ *Avenida Infante Dom Henrique/Cais da Pedra, Armazém B, Loja 7 • Map R3 • 218 877 532 • Open daily • €€*

3 D'Avis
Well-prepared food from the Alentejo region is on the menu at this tavern. Try dishes of *porco preto*, flavourful free-range Iberian pig. ⊗ *Rua do Grilo 96–8 • Map C2 • 218 681 354 • Closed Sun • €€€*

4 Casa do Leão
Housed in the remains of the original Alcáçovas castle (see p9) is this grand restaurant with an ambitious Portuguese menu. Sit outside, with Lisbon at your feet. ⊗ *Castelo de São Jorge • Map N3 • 218 875 962 • Open L & D daily • €€€€*

5 Arco do Castelo
Genuine Goan restaurants like this one are now quite a rarity. Try spicy specialities like *sarapatel*, *balchão de porco* or chicken *xacuti*. ⊗ *Rua Chão da Feira 25 • Map N4 • 218 876 598 • Closed Sun • €*

6 Faz Figura
There are wonderful views of the river from the large terrace of this stylish eatery. The menu includes international dishes. ⊗ *Rua do Paraíso 15b • Map R3 • 218 868 981 • Open daily • €€€€*

7 Mercado de Santa Clara
Upstairs in an old market hall, on the square hosting a flea market every Tuesday and Saturday, this friendly place has quality Portuguese cooking. ⊗ *Campo de Santa Clara • Map Q2 • 218 869 163 • Closed Tue • €€€*

8 Lautasco
Traditional Portuguese fare is the speciality of this informal restaurant, rustically decorated with wooden panelling. ⊗ *Beco do Azinhal 7A (off Rua de São Pedro) • Map Q4 • 218 860 173 • Closed Sun • €€€*

9 Santo António de Alfama
Not as traditional as the name and location would suggest: the walls are lined with black-and-white portraits of film stars, but the food is modern Portuguese and international. ⊗ *Beco de São Miguel 7 • Map P4 • 218 881 328 • Open daily • €€€*

10 Viagem de Sabores
Choose this charming old restaurant's "tastes journey" for a small but varied selection of dishes from all over the world. Strong on starters. ⊗ *Rua de São João da Praça 103 • Map P5 • 218 870 189 • Open D daily, closed Sun • €€€*

Left **Bronze statue of King João I, Praça da Figuiera** Right **Praça do Comércio**

Baixa to Restauradores

FROM THE EARLY 16th to mid-18th centuries, Lisbon's royal palace stood on the riverbank, around today's Praça do Comércio. It was the grand entrance to Lisbon, one of the world's great cities. Then in 1755 the earth shook, the ocean rose and fires raged – and the Paço Real and most of the medieval jumble of buildings behind it were gone. The Baixa we see was built on the ruins of lower Lisbon, to a different plan, in a different style, for a new era. Today this is the ageing heart of Lisbon, challenged by depopulation, traffic, subsidence and shopping centres – but still loved and alive.

Triumphal arch, Rua Augusta, with Praça do Comércio beyond

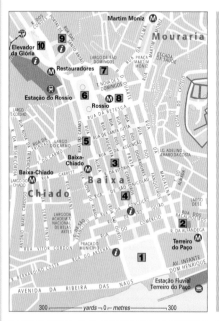

🔟 Sights

1 Praça do Comércio

2 Igreja da Conceição Velha

3 Rua Augusta

4 Núcleo Arqueológico da Rua dos Correeiros

5 Elevador de Santa Justa

6 Rossio

7 Igreja de São Domingos

8 Praça da Figueira

9 Rua das Portas de Santo Antão

🔟 Praça dos Restauradores

1 Praça do Comércio

The broad riverfront square also known as Terreiro do Paço has regained some of its stature since cars were prohibited from parking there. Surrounded on three sides by the elegant arcades of Pombal's reconstruction (see p31), and facing the river along the fourth, this is an urban space whose beauty is still crying out for a true role in the city. Dom José I, Portugal's ineffectual king at the time of the earthquake, gazes – perhaps fearfully – at the river from his horseback perch in bronze, by Machado de Castro. ◈ Map M5

2 Igreja da Conceição Velha

This was the grand 16th-century Igreja da Misericórdia before the 1755 earthquake, which destroyed everything but the Manueline portal and one interior chapel. When it opened again in 1770, it was taken over by the congregation of another Baixa church that had been irreparably damaged in the quake, the Conceição Velha. The new church was very modest, and most visitors today come to admire the detailed portal. This features a carved image of Our Lady of Mercy, her long mantle held by two angels to shelter kneeling historical figures including Dom Manuel, Pope Leo X and Dona Leonor, widow of João II and founder of the Misericórdia almshouses. ◈ Rua da Alfândega • Map N5 • Open 8am–6pm Mon–Fri; Sun for services only

Carved angel, Igreja da Conceição Velha

3 Rua Augusta

Lisbon's longest and grandest pedestrianized street runs from one corner of Rossio through the middle of Baixa to a triumphal archway on Praça de Comércio. The arch, which commemorates the city's recovery after the 1755 earthquake, was added only in 1873. An allegorical figure of Glory stands atop it, crowning figures representing Genius and Bravery with wreaths. The gallery of national heroes below these includes the Marquis of Pombal. The side facing Rua Augusta features a large clock, much used by the shoppers who throng the street. ◈ Map M4–5

4 Núcleo Arqueológico da Rua dos Correeiros

When a Portuguese bank (now Millennium BCP) began renovating its head office in the early 1990s, the builders' jack-hammers unearthed ancient remnants of Roman Lisbon. A small museum was set up, and the digging goes on. So far, this has revealed parts of what appears to have been a riverside factory for making garum, the fermented fish sauce much loved by the Romans. A section of mosaic floor uncovered in a separate structure suggests other, or later uses. ◈ Rua dos Correeiros 9 • Map M4 • Guided tours in English: Thu 3–5pm; Sat 10am–noon; book in advance: 211 131 000

Rua Augusta

Praça Dom Pedro IV, Rossio

Elevador de Santa Justa

You may be told that this iron lift was designed by Eiffel (of the Paris tower fame), but in fact it is by Raoul Mesnier de Ponsard, his Portuguese pupil. There were once three such lifts in Lisbon's craggy cityscape, before the era of small delivery lorries. Today the Neo-Gothic lift (look at the sides of the tower) whisks lazy types and tourists from Baixa to the Carmo ruin *(see p71)*. There are photo opportunities and a scenic terrace at the top. ✎ *Rua de Santa Justa • Map M4 • Runs 7am–11pm summer, 7am–9pm winter • Bus/tram ticket*

"Only the pigeons will see it isn't him ... "

The statue atop the column in Rossio of course represents Dom Pedro IV, the king who gave his (unwanted) name to the square. But is it actually him? It's said to be of Emperor Maximilian of Mexico, whose bronze likeness was in transit in Lisbon when news came through that he had been assassinated. Since the city fathers – after much argument over the expense – had just ordered a bronze of Dom Pedro IV from the same French sculptor, agreement was reached to substitute, at cut price, the now superfluous Maximilian. This served everyone's purposes. Except Dom Pedro's, that is.

Rossio

Rossio, officially but rarely called Praça Dom Pedro IV, has been Lisbon's main square for as long as anyone can remember. Probably for longer: Roman Olisipo's hippodrome is said to have been here. Surrounded by some of the city's grandest buildings before the earthquake, it was outshone by the new Praça do Comércio after the reconstruction – but has yet to cede its position as the city's cosmopolitan, coffee-fuelled heart. ✎ *Praça Dom Pedro IV • Map L3–M3*

Igreja de São Domingos

Dark and cavernous, the São Domingos church is not much visited by tourists, despite its long history. As a result, it is a good place for quiet reflection, whatever one's creed *(see p32).*

Praça da Figueira

After the earthquake, even as the rubble of the vast Hospital Real de Todos-os-Santos was being cleared, an open-air market was set up in what is now Praça da Figueira. It became the city's main vegetable market, and eventually was roofed with iron pavilions and cupolas. Praça da Figueira joined next-door Rossio as Lisbon's bustling centre, scene of raucous Santo António celebrations in mid-June. Sadly, it is today a bleak shadow of its former self, serving as the vented lid of an underground car park, forlornly bestridden by an equestrian Dom João I looking for action. However, there are broad, shaded café esplanades along one side, and the square looks quite attractive when viewed from up on the castle ramparts. ✎ *Map M3*

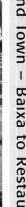

9 Rua das Portas de Santo Antão

This long, partly pedestrianized street has food for everyone. The legendary Gambrinus restaurant is next door to the tiny Ginjinha Sem Rival bar, and between these extremes is a rash of seafood restaurants with outdoor seating, plus the atmospheric Casa do Alentejo, the cheerful Bomjardim, and the inimitable Solmar *(see pp68–9)*. ⊗ Map L2

10 Praça dos Restauradores

This plaza and its monument were built when the old Passeio Público was turned into Avenida da Liberdade in the 1870s. It commemorates the restoration of the Portuguese monarchy in 1640. The obelisk is engraved with important dates from the restoration campaign, and is flanked by statues representing the Spirit of Independence and Victory. The surrounding square is dominated by traffic; shops, cafés, kiosks and restaurants cluster in its lower corners. ⊗ Map L2

Monument to the Restoration, Praça dos Restauradores

A Stroll through Baixa

Morning

Begin at the river's edge in **Praça do Comércio**, where the old palace steps can still be seen. Cross the street at the right-hand corner of the square and head up under the arcades. Turning right on Rua da Alfândega, take in the Manueline portal of **Igreja da Conceição Velha**. To refuel, the café **Castella do Paulo** is on the same street as the church. Then head up Rua da Madalena, where you can drop into the **Conserveira de Lisboa** *(see p66)* if you happen to fancy some tinned Portuguese sardines. Turn left at Largo da Madalena and descend two blocks to the narrower **Rua dos Douradores**, haunt of Fernando Pessoa's troubled alter ego in *The Book of Disquietude*. Here you will find plenty of restaurants to choose from for lunch.

Afternoon

After lunch, work your way through Baixa's grid, zig-zagging between whatever shops catch your eye. Next stop is the top left corner of **Praça da Figueira**, and a coffee outside the back of **Casa Suíça** *(see p68)*. Then walk up **Rua Dom Antão de Almada**, past fragrant shops selling herbs and other dried goods. On your right is one of Lisbon's oldest churches, **Igreja de São Domingos** *(see p32)*. Slightly left and then straight ahead is **Rua das Portas de Santo Antão**. If you've already worked up an appetite, you couldn't be in a better street; and for a pre-prandial drink, you could do worse than duck into the tiny **Ginjinha Sem Rival** bar *(see p68)* for a morello-cherry liqueur.

Left **Teatro Nacional Dona Maria II by night** Right **Detail of arch over Rossio Station entrance**

🔟 Best of the Rest

1 Elevador do Lavra
The oldest Lisbon funicular, inaugurated in 1884, is the one most tourists miss. Connecting Restauradores with Campo de Santana, it gets you to the Torel viewpoint *(see p37)*. 🖎 *Largo da Anunciada/Calçada do Lavra • Map L1*

2 Rossio Station
Built in 1892, the old central station now serves Sintra *(see pp26–7)*. The statue in a niche between the horseshoe arches is of Dom Sebastião, the boy king lost in battle in 1578. 🖎 *Between Rossio and Restauradores squares • Map L3*

3 Shops in Rua do Arsenal
A whiff of an older Lisbon lives on in shops selling dried fish, from *bacalhau* (salt cod) to octopus, other dried goods, wine and some fresh produce. 🖎 *Map L5*

4 Museu do Design e da Moda (MUDE)
This fine museum showcases 20th-century design and fashion pieces from around the world. 🖎 *Rua Augusta 24 • Map M5 • 218 886 117 • Open 10am–8pm Tue–Thu, 10am–10pm Fri & Sat*

5 Teatro Nacional Dona Maria II
The Neo-Classical building housing Portugal's national theatre was built around 1840, at the same time as Rossio was paved with its characteristic black and white cobblestones. 🖎 *Praça Dom Pedro IV • Map L3 • 213 250 800*

6 Haberdashers in Rua da Conceição
Baixa shopkeepers are buckling under competition from shopping centres; haberdashers are among the more resilient. At this string of shops you can buy a single button or a length of lace. 🖎 *Between Rua Augusta and Rua da Prata • Map M5*

7 Antiga Ervanária d'Anunciada
Herbalists have always had a strong following in Portugal. This shop claims to be the country's oldest, and sells vitamin super-cures as well as traditional dried herbs for infusions. 🖎 *Largo da Anunciada 13–15 • Map L2 • 213 427 997*

8 Shoeshiners in Largo de São Domingos
The *engraxador* is an emblematic Lisbon figure, much stereotyped in literature and film, but his is a fading trade. The surest place to find one is outside (or inside) the Ginjinha bar *(see p68)*. Expect to pay at least €1. 🖎 *Map M3*

9 Arte Rústica
This shop is well stocked with the most popular regional crafts, particularly hand-painted ceramics and embroidery. 🖎 *Rua do Ouro 246–8 • Map M4 • 213 421 127*

10 Conserveira de Lisboa
This charming wholesaler of tinned fish, especially sardines, is the kind of place that makes Baixa a living museum. 🖎 *Rua dos Bacalhoeiros 34 • Map N5 • 218 864 009*

Left **Vitorino de Sousa (tanner)** Right **Napoleão wines**

🔟 Shops

Azevedo Rua
The famous hatter at the northeastern corner of Rossio has managed to stay in business for 120 years despite the vagaries of hat-wearing fashions. ✎ *Praça Dom Pedro IV 69 • Map M3 • 213 427 511*

Manuel Tavares
A tourist-oriented, but good, deli between Rossio and Praça da Figueira, where wine, cheese and ham may sometimes be tasted before purchase. ✎ *Rua da Betesga 1 • Map M3 • 213 424 209*

Napoleão
This branch of a wine-shop chain offers friendly, personalized service and a wide choice of table and fortified wines, as well as some spirits. ✎ *Rua dos Fanqueiros 70 • Map N5 • 218 872 042*

Santos Ofícios
The city's best shop for handicrafts and folk art has a selection that extends well beyond the run of the mill, particularly in terms of imaginative figures made from a variety of materials. ✎ *Rua da Madalena 87 • Map N4 • 218 872 031*

Vitorino de Sousa
The only remaining tanner's in "Tanners' Street", Vitorino de Sousa sells boots, saddles and bridles, plus other equestrian and country gear. Its leather goods are handmade to order and can be shipped. ✎ *Rua dos Correeiros 200 • Map M4 • 213 427 458*

Hospital de Bonecas
The doll's hospital is not much bigger than a doll's house, but full of perfectly healthy dolls, as well as clothes and furniture for them. Barbie is not much in evidence. Dried herbs are also sold here. ✎ *Praça da Figueira 7 • Map M3 • 213 428 574*

Pollux
Round the back of the many-floored, much-maligned Pollux department store, this shop sells excellent Portuguese stainless-steel cookware, knives and other serious cooking aids. ✎ *Rua da Madalena 251 • Map M4 • 218 811 200*

Discoteca Amália
Not a disco, but a "disc shop" specializing in traditional Portuguese music. It's not all *fado*, even if it's mostly *fado*; and *fado* isn't only Amália Rodrigues, even if it's mostly her. ✎ *Rua do Ouro 272 • Map M4 • 213 463 165*

Lisbonense
At this old-school shoe shop styles are traditional, good value and sport an inner label to remind you of Lisbon. It specializes in orthopaedic shoes. ✎ *Rua Augusta 202 • Map M4 • 213 426 712*

Joalharia Correia
This jeweller's is the place for cutting, replacing and repairing semi-precious and precious gems. The shop reflects the family's colonial African background. ✎ *Rua do Ouro 245–7 • Map M4 • 213 427 384*

Left **A Licorista** Centre **Nicola** Right **Café Martinho da Arcada**

Bars and Cafés

Nicola
Rossio's premier outdoor café is well sited for people-watching. It has a venerable history and a handsome marble Art-Deco interior. Downstairs, there is a restaurant. Coffee is cheapest at the bar; most expensive outside.
❧ *Praça Dom Pedro IV 24 • Map L3*

Casa Suiça
Opposite Nicola across the square, and its main competitor, Suiça has a shorter history but a longer, narrower esplanade and a wider selection of pastries and snacks. Lunch and dinner are served as well, but only indoors.
❧ *Praça Dom Pedro IV 96–104 • Map M3*

Confeitaria Nacional
A Lisbon institution for a Portuguese passion: cakes and pastries. It offers a busy take-away service and café tables inside under a mirror-clad ceiling.
❧ *Praça da Figueira 18 • Map M3*

A Licorista
A vaulted-brick ceiling gives this rustic bar and restaurant a rather grand frame. The next-door restaurant, O Bacalhoeiro *(see p69)*, has the same owners.
❧ *Rua dos Sapateiros 218 • Map M4*

British Bar
At what was once the Taverna Inglesa, haunt of Brits from local shipping firms, the selection of beers is wider than usual. The wall clock ticks anticlockwise.
❧ *Rua Bernardino Costa 52 • Map L6*

VIP Eden
Head-spinning views of the castle and downtown Lisbon are the main draw at this secret café at the top of the VIP Executive Suites Eden hotel *(see p117)*. Just ask at reception and press T for "terrace" in the elevator.
❧ *Praça dos Restauradores 24 • Map L2*

Café Martinho da Arcada
Attractively tiled in blue and white, this bustling café serves good-value lunches at the counter. A few tables are arranged inside; there are more outside under the arcades.
The restaurant next door is more famous *(see opposite)*, but this is a quintessential Lisbon location.
❧ *Praça do Comércio 3 • Map N5*

Néctar Wine Bar
Lovers of fine wine and port can choose from an eclectic range at this chic but unpretentious bar and restaurant.
❧ *Rua dos Douradores 33 • Map M4*

A Ginjinha
Ginjinha is Portuguese cherry liqueur and this tiny bar serves virtually nothing else. A Ginjinha has survived for over 150 years on sheer single-mindedness.
❧ *Largo de São Domingos 8 • Map M3*

O'Gilins
Lisbon's first Irish pub is still the city's best, popular with students and expats alike. There is live music at weekends.
❧ *Rua dos Remolares 8 • Map K6*

An espresso is known in Lisbon as a bica; *a café au lait is a* meia de leite.

Price Categories

For a three course meal for one with half a bottle of wine (or equivalent meal), taxes and extra charges.

€€€€
€€€€€ over

Casa do Alentejo

🔟 Restaurants

1 Valentino Restauradores
Reasonably priced and with plenty of outdoor seating, this is one of the best Italian restaurants in downtown Lisbon. Try the freshly made ravioli or the pepperoni pizza. ⓢ *Rua Jardim do Regedor 37 • Map L2 • 213 461 727 • €€*

2 Gambrinus
This classic Lisbon address is as famous for its seafood dishes and "rich fish soup" as it is for its high prices and endless business lunches. ⓢ *Rua das Portas de Santo Antão 23 • Map L2 • 213 421 466 • €€€€€*

3 Martinho da Arcada
Once a favourite of literary figures such as Fernando Pessoa, this is a good place to eat traditional Portuguese food in the right kind of setting (though outside it is noisy). ⓢ *Praça do Comércio 3 • Map M5 • 218 879 259 • Closed Sun • €€€*

4 O Bacalhoeiro
This cosy restaurant is named after the Portuguese trawlers that fished cod off the coast of Newfoundland, then salted it on board. Don't miss the *bacalhau* here. ⓢ *Rua dos Sapateiros 220 • Map M4 • 213 431 415 • Closed Sun • €€*

5 Alfândega – Armazém dos Sabores
Light, Mediterranean-style dishes are served in a pleasant, colourful space next door to the Conceição church *(see p63)*. ⓢ *Rua da Alfândega 98 • Map N5 • 218 861 683 • Closed Sat L, Sun, Mon D • €€*

6 Leão d'Ouro
This cathedral-like restaurant is indeed a temple: to fish. Superfresh specimens are on display to draw custom. ⓢ *Rua 1 Dezembro 105 • Map L3 • 213 426 195 • €€€€*

7 Casa do Alentejo
This Neo-Moorish former palace is home to an association for people from the Alentejo region. The restaurant is open to the public and serves simple Alentejan food in a choice of memorable rooms. ⓢ *Rua das Portas de Santo Antão 58 (upstairs) • Map L2 • 213 405 140 • €*

8 Bonjardim Rei dos Frangos
Grilled chicken with *piri-piri* (chilli) is one of the fondest food memories many visitors take away from Portugal: this is one of the best purveyors. ⓢ *Travessa de Santo Antão 7–11 • Map L2 • 213 427 424 • €*

9 Cervejaria Solmar
This classic Lisbon seafood restaurant has a wonderfully unmodernized 1950s setting. *Cervejarias* (beer halls) are also informal restaurants that often do seafood. ⓢ *Rua das Portas de Santo Antão 106 • Map L2 • 213 230 098 • €€€*

10 Varanda de Lisboa
Great views of the Baixa can be enjoyed from the top of Hotel Mundial, whose restaurant serves a fairly classic hotel menu with a Portuguese accent. ⓢ *Hotel Mundial, Praça Martim Moniz 2 • Map M3 • 218 842 000 • €€€€*

Left **Museu do Chiado** Right **Calçada do Duque**

Chiado & Bairro Alto

CHIADO IS WHERE SOME OF LISBON'S OLDER HILLS, *steeped in history, collided with the new cartography of Pombal's reconstructed city centre;* and sparks flew, for a century at least. Today, both areas are old and venerated, and full of shops, but Chiado's history and cultural institutions give its commercial activities a gilt edge. Higher up is Bairro Alto – the "high

neighbourhood" – a 16th-century maze of narrow streets framed by the wider lanes and longer blocks of later construction. It is best known as the district of Lisbon with the highest concentration of bars, but it is also a residential area and, at its western end, a quiet neighbourhood of grand old mansions.

Praça Luís de Camões

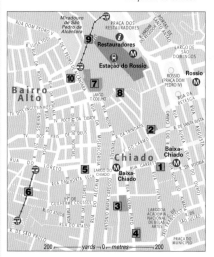

Sights

1. Rua do Carmo and Rua Garrett
2. Largo and Convento do Carmo
3. Teatro Nacional de São Carlos
4. Museu do Chiado
5. Praça Luís de Camões
6. Elevador da Bica
7. Igreja e Museu de São Roque
8. Calçada do Duque
9. Elevador da Glória
10. Solar do Vinho do Porto

For more on the Marquis of Pombal See p31

1 Rua do Carmo and Rua Garrett

Chiado's main arteries flow at right angles to each other, meeting in front of Armazéns do Chiado, a shopping centre housed in the shell of a famed department store destroyed by a fire in 1988. These partially pedestrianized, mildly to steeply inclined streets are among Lisbon's most bustling, and are lined with shops old and new. Walkers up from Baixa are rewarded at the top, where the classic café A Brasileira *(see p75)* awaits. ⊗ *Map L4*

2 Largo and Convento do Carmo

Accessible from Baixa using the Elevador de Santa Justa *(see p64)*, the ruin of the 14th-century Carmo church acts as a memorial to the 1755 earthquake. Look at the repaired rupture in one of the arches and ponder the fact that the whole structure didn't collapse. The quiet square in front of the church, littered with jacaranda blossom fallen from the trees in spring, seems an unlikely setting for one of the most dramatic events in recent Portuguese history. It was here that army tanks threatened the barracks of the National Guard, next door to the Carmo church, where Marcelo Caetano, the country's dictator, had taken refuge on 25 April 1974. His surrender ended 42 years of fascist dictatorship in Portugal. ⊗ *Map L4*
• *Carmo ruin open 10am–7pm Mon–Sat (10am–6pm winter)* • *Closed Sun*
• *Adm charge*

Carmo church, detail of carved stone cherub

3 Teatro Nacional de São Carlos

Lisbon's opera house dates from 1793, and is regarded as the city's first Neo-Classical building. Its grand façade – the only side of the building decorated, in keeping with post-earthquake regulations – takes its cue from Milan's La Scala. But the floor plan resembles that of Naples' San Carlo opera, since destroyed in a fire. The grand interior owes more to the Baroque, with the gilt wood, marble and plush typical of opera houses. There is a café and restaurant with tables in the square *(see p75)*. ⊗ *Rua Serpa Pinto 9* • *Map L5* • *213 253 045* • *Box office open 1–7pm Mon–Fri* • *Ticket prices vary* • *www.saocarlos.pt*

4 Museu do Chiado

One of Chiado's heavyweight cultural institutions, located in the same block as the Academy of Fine Arts, the Chiado Museum is nonetheless an unfusty place for viewing Portuguese art from the mid-19th century on. The core collection covers about 1850–1950, but recent acquisitions and temporary shows bring things up to date. ⊗ *Rua Serpa Pinto 4* • *Map L5* • *Open 10am–6pm Tue–Sun* • *Adm charge* • *www.museudochiado-ipmuseus.pt*

Teatro Nacional de São Carlos

 The Chiado Museum has a good café.

Lisbon's Liver

Bairro Alto's association with bohemian lifestyles, loose living and drinking goes back several centuries (drug-dealing is a more recent feature). Even when the area was a posh residential district in the 17th and 18th centuries – and parts of it still are – there was a shadier side. In the 19th century, newspaper offices and printing shops moved in, bringing with them a demand for cheap and somewhat unrefined entertainment. In 1833, the local authorities decided to make Bairro Alto a zone of regulated prostitution. Fado singing was closely associated with all this; today's tidied-up version is really a sort of *fado bourgeois*.

Praça Luís de Camões

This square, where Chiado meets Bairro Alto, is a favourite rendezvous. It is named after the poet laureate, whose heroic bronze, with lesser chroniclers and colleagues in stone around his feet, presides over the bright white stone oval traffic island. It used to be shaded by magnificent umbrella pines, but these have been replaced – supposedly for reasons of historical consistency – by still-puny poplars. ✆ *Map K4*

Elevador da Bica

Opened in 1892, this is the smallest of Lisbon's funiculars, passing through the lively neighbourhood of Bica on its way between Largo do Calhariz and Rua de São Paulo. Like Lisbon's other funiculars, it is powered by an electric motor, which moves the cable to which both cars are attached; they counterbalance each other and so lighten the motor's load. ✆ *Largo do Calhariz at Rua da Bica Duarte Belo • Map K4 • Runs 7am–9pm Mon–Sat, 9am–9pm Sun & public holidays • Bus/tram ticket*

Igreja e Museu de São Roque

The Jesuit church of St Roch, built in the second half of the 16th century on the edge of what would become Bairro Alto, is a monument to the wealth of religious orders and to the extravagance of Dom João V – although you wouldn't know it from the outside. Inside, however, its chapel to St John the Baptist has been described as one of the most expensive ever made. It was assembled in Rome in the 1740s, from all the most precious materials available at the time, then disassembled and shipped to Lisbon to be put back together again. The church's Museum of Sacred Art, with further riches from the chapel, has an impressive collection of vestments and paintings *(see p33)*.

Calçada do Duque

This series of steps, from Largo Trindade Coelho to the bottom of Calçada do Carmo, is a treat. Along the

Elevador da Bica

Tile detail, Igreja de São Roque

gradual descent are Café Buenos Aires *(see p77)* and a number of other restaurants. The view of the Castle, foreshortened above Rossio, is perfectly framed. ◈ *Map L3*

Elevador da Glória
Lisbon's best-known and now its busiest funicular links Restauradores with Bairro Alto. The second to be built, it was inaugurated in 1885 after lengthy discussion. Formerly, the cars were open-top double- deckers, propelled by cog-rail and cable, with a water counterweight. Later on, steam power was used, but in 1915 the Glória went electric.
◈ *Praça dos Restauradores at Calçada da Glória • Map K3 • Runs 7am–midnight Mon–Thu, 7am–2am Fri, 8:30am–2am Sat, 9am–midnight Sun • Bus/tram ticket*

Solar do Vinho do Porto
This cool, lounge-like bar has existed for many years. The impressive wine list becomes rather shorter when you start to order, but be patient; some of the waiters have been in reserve longer than the older wines – and still manage to remain utterly unpassionate about port.
◈ *Rua de São Pedro de Alcântara 45 • Map K3 • Open 11am–midnight Mon–Fri, 2pm–midnight Sat*

Chiado to Bairro Alto and the Bica

Morning

Begin by the **Carmo** ruin – reached, if you're coming from Baixa, via the Elevador de Santa Justa. Crossing to the bottom-left-hand corner of the square, take Travessa do Carmo, stopping for coffee at **Vertigo** *(see p75)*.

Cross Largo Rafael Bordalo Pinheiro to Rua da Trindade and then Rua Nova da Trindade, on which turn right. Passing the famous **Cevejaria Trindade** on the right, you soon reach the top of **Calçada do Duque**. Straight ahead is **Igreja de São Roque**. Past the church, the street leads to the top of the **Elevador da Glória** on your left, and the **Solar do Vinho do Porto** on your right. For lunch, carry on up the street (here called Rua Dom Pedro V) and try **Tapas Bar** at no.52, or **La Paparrucha** at no.18 – an Argentinian steak house with great city views.

Afternoon

After lunch, stroll and shop at your leisure in Bairro Alto, entering via **Rua da Rosa** on the other side of Rua Dom Pedro V. Meander, but keep track of Rua da Rosa, which will take you out of the area on the other side. Here, across the street, is the top of the **Elevador da Bica**. Ride it down to Rua de São Paulo and then head left towards Cais do Sodré and a drink at **O'Gilin's** or **The British Bar** *(see p68)*. Otherwise, you can walk halfway up the steep hill again and turn left into one of the narrow streets which will take you to **Miradouro de Santa Catarina** *(see p36)* and afternoon refreshments in the open air, overlooking the river.

Left **Livraria Bertrand** Centre **Luvaria Ulisses** Right **José António Tenente**

Shops

1 Luvaria Ulisses
This small gem of a shop is the only one in Portugal selling just gloves. Hand sewn, they have a lifetime guarantee for repairs. ® *Rua do Carmo 87A • Map L4*

2 Leitão & Irmão
Jewellery and silverware from a company that was appointed crown jewellers in 1875. The pieces are kept in museums and private collections the world over and at a shop in Lisbon's Ritz hotel. ® *Largo do Chiado 16 • Map L4*

3 A Carioca
Coffee beans from Africa, Asia and South America are roasted on the premises and sold either freshly ground or whole. Tea and chocolate are also available; try the chocolate from São Tomé. ® *Rua da Misericórdia 9 • Map L4*

4 José António Tenente
The well-known Portuguese clothes designer José António Tenente produced his first collection in 1989 and opened his first boutique in 1990. This is his flagship shop. ® *Travessa do Carmo 8 • Map L4*

5 Vista Alegre
The work of Portugal's premier porcelain maker is wide ranging: from modern to traditional designs, and from restrained tableware to exuberant decorative pieces. ® *Largo do Chiado 20–21 • Map L4*

6 Ana Salazar
Hailing from Lisbon, Ana Salazar transformed Portuguese fashion in the 1970s and is an internationally acclaimed stylist, arguably the country's best. ® *Rua do Carmo 87 • Map L4*

7 Storytailors
This store showcases the talents of young stylists João Branco and Luís Sanchez, whose sense of glamour embraces a fairy-tale theme. ® *Calçada do Ferragial 8 • Map L5*

8 Agência 117
One of the first alternative fashion shops in Lisbon is a place both for browsing and for hanging out. There are own-label, Jocomomola and Custo Barcelona clothes, as well as Fly London shoes. ® *Rua do Norte 117 • Map K4*

9 Armazéns do Chiado
In the carefully restored shell of what was Lisbon's poshest department store – destroyed by fire in 1988 – is the city's most central shopping centre. Larger retailers include FNAC and Sport Zone. Check out the food court for some great views. ® *Rua do Carmo 2 • Map L4*

10 Livraria Bertrand
The Bertrand chain has branches all over the city; this one is Lisbon's oldest bookshop. In its warren of rooms it stocks a wide selection of English-language titles. ® *Rua Garrett 73 • Map L4*

Left **A Brasileira** Right **Cafetaria de São Carlos**

Chiado: Cafés

1 A Brasileira
The city's most famous café is an Art Nouveau tunnel of florid stuccowork, mirrors and paintings from its 1920s heyday. The tables outside, where a bronze of poet Fernando Pessoa still lingers today, are among Lisbon's most coveted. ⊗ *Rua Garrett 120 • Map L4*

2 Bénard
For many this is "the other café" next to A Brasileira. In fact, it is a tearoom with cakes and pastries superior to those of its neighbour. Its outdoor tables serve as a welcome extension to A Brasileira's often crowded terrace. ⊗ *Rua Garrett 104 • Map L4*

3 No Chiado
This tranquil café is just a block from the bustle of Rua Garrett, but a world away. Al fresco tables, Internet access and light meals are all available. ⊗ *Largo do Picadeiro 12 • Map L5*

4 Royale
Organic light lunches, snacks and cakes are served in this elegant café, which has a small interior courtyard. Service is friendly. ⊗ *Largo Rafael Bordalo Pinheiro 29 • Map L4*

5 Leitaria Académica
This venerable milk bar is named after Lisbon's first university. Its outdoor tables in peaceful Largo do Carmo are popular. Hearty meals are also served. ⊗ *Largo do Carmo 1 • Map L4*

6 Sacramento
This place is a warren of rooms on different levels, all pleasantly cool, with whitewashed walls and bare-brick arches. The café overlooks the street; there is also a restaurant and a club. ⊗ *Calçada do Sacramento 40 • Map L4*

7 Vertigo
A warm ambience permeates this café, whose heavy-framed mirrors and stained wood give it an old-style feel. Its informal service and organic snacks are, however, bang up-to-date. ⊗ *Travessa do Carmo 4 • Map L4*

8 Cafetaria de São Carlos
Next to the São Carlos opera house *(see p71)* is a square that was once used as a parking lot. Now, one corner of it is a permanent terrace for the opera's restaurant and café – another peaceful Chiado perch. ⊗ *Largo São Carlos 23 • Map L5*

9 Kaffeehaus
This busy café-bar adds a delightful dash of Vienna to the Portuguese capital. Bag an outside table in the sun for coffee and apple strudel. ⊗ *Rua Anchieta 3 • Map L5*

10 Chá do Carmo
Located on a tranquil square in front of the Carmo ruins, this café offers several types of tea. The lunch menu has hot dishes, salads and home-made desserts. ⊗ *Largo do Carmo 21 • Map L4*

Left **Portas Largas** Right **Bedroom**

🔟 Bairro Alto: Bars

Artis
1 Artis is one of Bairro Alto's most lived-in bars. It's a great place for those who like low lights, the sound of jazz, late conversation and toasted chicken sandwiches. ✆ *Rua Diário de Notícias 95 • Map K4*

Bedroom
2 At this DJ bar the aim is to break with minimalism by furnishing the interior with comfortable beds, patterned wallpaper and clever lighting. The music is hip-hop, electro and tracks from the 1980s and 1990s. ✆ *Rua do Norte 86 • Map K4*

Portas Largas
3 This is the Bairro Alto in a nutshell. "Wide Doors", as it is called, is a rustic-tavern-turned-bar, whose party spills out onto the street. It is gay, but not overwhelmingly so. ✆ *Rua Atalaia 105 • Map K3*

Capela
4 The decor of this DJ bar combines sparseness with extravagance. The deep yet narrow space can get extremely crowded – but always with an interesting mix of people. ✆ *Rua da Atalaia 45 • Map K4*

Catacumbas
5 This is a highly civilized, café-like jazz bar. There is live music occasionally; customers sometimes play the piano too. ✆ *Travessa Água da Flor 43 • Map K3*

Clube da Esquina
6 Well on the way to classic status, the "Corner Club" is a chatty, crowded, yet relaxed place whose well-lit interior with exposed wooden beams has framed many a good start to a Bairro Alto night. ✆ *Rua da Barroca 30 • Map K4*

Salto Alto
7 Housed in a former milk-production building dating back to 1836, Salto Alto caters for a mixed crowd with a rich assortment of pop, chill-out and electronic music from Thursday to Saturday. Smoking is permitted. ✆ *Rua Rosa 159 • Map K3*

Etílico
8 Comfy sofas and a varied group of resident DJs are assets of this brightly coloured DJ bar with a friendly vibe. ✆ *Rua do Grémio Lusitano 8 • Map K3*

Aché Cohiba
9 Lisbon's liveliest Cuban bar promises a real taste of Havana, with frenzied DJ sessions, deadly cocktails and some of the whackiest staff you'll ever meet. ✆ *Rua do Norte 121 • Map K4*

Pavilhão Chinês
10 Among the oldest bars in Bairro Alto, this place has something completely different. Its series of rooms is decorated with collections of dolls, Airfix models, hats, coasters and the like. ✆ *Rua Dom Pedro V 89 • Map K2*

The best streets for bar-hopping are Rua da Atalaia, Rua da Barroca, Rua do Diário de Notícias and Rua do Norte.

Price Categories

For a three course meal for one with half a bottle of wine (or equivalent meal), taxes and extra charges.		
€	under €15
€€	€15–€20
€€€	€20–€30
€€€€	€30–€40
€€€€€	over €40

Tavares

⑩ Restaurants

Tavares
1 Lisbon's oldest restaurant has an ornate Edwardian interior with gilded wood, stucco and red plush. The underlyingly Portuguese menu has been reignited by French chef Philippe Peudenier *(see p45)*.

Pap'Açorda
2 *Açorda (see p46)* is a rustic dish of the Alentejo region, here successfully modernized and glamourized. The rest of the menu also seasons tradition with a dash of innovation. It's a Lisbon classic. ✆ *Rua da Atalaia 57–9 • Map K4 • 213 464 811 • Closed Sun, Mon • €€€€*

100 Maneiras
3 Quality and creativity characterize the cuisine at this respected but low-key eatery on one of Bairro Alto's quietest blocks. Try the excellent tasting menu. ✆ *Rua do Teixeira 35 • Map K3 • 210 990 475 • Closed L daily; Sun • €€€€*

Alecrim às Flores
4 There are tables on the steps outside this friendly place. The mainly Portuguese dishes have a modern touch. Lamb is a good option. ✆ *Travessa do Alecrim 4 • Map K5 • 213 225 368 • Closed Sat L • €€€*

Largo
5 A noted gastronomic landmark, this fashionable and contemporary restaurant has a striking setting within the cloisters of the former Igreja dos Mártires. ✆ *Rua Serpa Pinto 10 • Map L5 • 213 477 225 • Closed Sun • €€€€*

Oriente
6 This reliable vegetarian restaurant has an appetizing buffet spread for lunch. It caters to vegans too. ✆ *Rua Ivens 28 • Map L4 • 910 465 849 • Closed Mon • €€*

Café Buenos Aires
7 On the steps between Bairro Alto and Rossio is this cosy Argentinian-inspired place with tables outside and a menu that is not all meat. ✆ *Calçada Escadinhas do Duque 31B • Map L3 • 213 420 739 • Closed Sun • €€*

Adega das Mercês
8 This classic Bairro Alto restaurant specializes in simple grilled fish and meat. Portions are traditionally generous – one is usually enough for two. ✆ *Travessa das Mercês 2 • Map K4 • 213 424 492 • Closed Sun • €€€*

Casanostra
9 One of Lisbon's first Italian restaurants remains one of its best, serving more than just good pasta. ✆ *Travessa do Poço da Cidade 60 • Map K4 • 213 425 931 • Closed Sat L • €€€*

Associação Católica Internacional ao Serviço da Juventude Feminina
10 A small roof-top terrace affords views of riverside Lisbon at this great lunch hideaway. It is open to the public – non-Catholics and men included. ✆ *Travessa do Ferragial 1 (2nd floor) • Map L5 • 213 240 910 • Closed D; Sat, Sun • €*

Left **Santo Amaro church** Right **Mosteiro Jerónimos, Belém**

West Lisbon

WEST LISBON COMPRISES A SERIES OF HILLS *on either side of the Alcântara valley, where a river once flowed but traffic now oozes onto the 25 de Abril bridge. The city's former aqueduct spans the valley, disappearing into the green expanse of the Monsanto Park on Lisbon's highest, broadest hill. Opposite Monsanto, the airy and desirable residential districts of Campo de Ourique, Estrela and Lapa descend in steep steps southwards towards the river. The waterfront from the Alcântara docks to Belém is a straight, accessible stretch bathed in bright light, with the 25 de Abril bridge arching overhead.*

Sights

1. Jardim Botânico
2. Casa Fernando Pessoa
3. Estrela
4. Assembleia da República
5. Museu de Arte Antiga
6. Museu da Marioneta
7. Ermida de Santo Amaro
8. Aqueduto das Águas Livres
9. Monsanto
10. Belém

Jardim Botânico

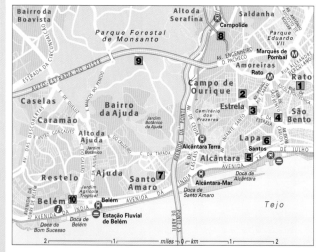

Preceding pages **The huge pavement compass in front of the Padrão dos Descobrimentos (Monument to the Discoveries)**

Jardim Botânico

Central Lisbon's sloping botanic garden was laid out in the second half of the 19th century, becoming the main showcase for exotic flora – taking over from Ajuda's botanic garden due to its more central location. Buildings at the top of the garden now house various museums, including an ageing but child-friendly Science Museum (see p51). ⌾ Rua da Escola Politécnica • Map J1–2 • 213 921 830 • Garden open 9am (10am Sat, Sun)–8pm (6pm in winter) • Adm charge

Casa Fernando Pessoa

Portugal's great modernist poet Fernando Pessoa lived in this building from 1920 until his death in 1935. Later acquired and comprehensively redesigned by the city council, in 1993 it opened as a museum dedicated to Pessoa and to poetry. It houses the poet's personal library, books about him, and a collection of Portuguese and foreign poetry. There is also a space for temporary exhibitions and events, some of Pessoa's furniture, and the poet's room, which was left unaltered and is "recreated" at irregular intervals by invited artists. A pleasant restaurant is set in the small modernist-style back garden. ⌾ Rua Coelho da Rocha 16–18 • Map E4 • 213 913 270 • Open 10am–6pm Mon– Sat • Free

Music pavilion, Jardim da Estrela

Estrela

The area between Campo de Ourique and Lapa takes its name from the Estrela basilica (see p32), opposite the entrance to central Lisbon's most agreeable park, Jardim da Estrela. It is also a distinctly British part of Lisbon, with the British embassy and English Cemetery (where Henry Fielding lies) close by. ⌾ Praça da Estrela • Map E4

Assembleia da República

This building has been the seat of the Portuguese parliament since 1833, when the Benedictine monks of the Convento de São Bento da Saúde were evicted – a year before the official dissolution of religious orders. The vast monastery was adapted in fits and starts; today's formal Neo-Classical building was designed at the end of the 19th century. In a city of hills and impressive prospects, it sits surprisingly humbly at the bottom of a hill. ⌾ Largo das Cortes • Map F4 • 213 919 625 • Visits by appointment only • Free

Assembleia da República

A Golden Gate for Europe

By the time the steel suspension bridge was built across the Tejo in 1962–6, bridges had been proposed at various sites for nearly a century. Similar in design to San Francisco's Golden Gate bridge, Ponte Salazar (as it was originally called, after Portugal's dictator) is just over 1km (over half a mile) long, making it Europe's longest bridge in 1966. Its two towers are just under 200m (650ft) tall. Renamed Ponte 25 de Abril of that date in 1974, it has been adapted to increasing traffic over the 40 years of its existence by squeezing in extra lanes and adding a railway crossing underneath the roadway. By the early 1990s, however, its traffic jams were getting notorious. The 1998 opening of the Vasco da Gama bridge (also briefly the longest in Europe) has taken some of the pressure off.

5 Museu de Arte Antiga

Portugal's national museum holds some of the country's greatest artistic treasures, as well as foreign masterpieces such as Bosch's *The Temptations of St Anthony* – not in fact St Anthony of Padua, one of Lisbon's patron saints, but the Egyptian St Anthony, founder of Christian monasticism *(see pp14–15)*.

6 Museu da Marioneta

Lisbon's Puppet Museum has a collection of over 800 puppets from all over the world, as well as scenery, props and machinery for puppet shows. It is housed in a former convent which it shares with housing and the gourmet restaurant A Travessa *(see p44)*. The museum also holds shows and puppet-making workshops for school groups. ✆ *Rua da Esperança 146 (Convento das Bernardas)* • *Map F5* • *213 942 810* • *Open 10am–12:30pm, 2–5:30pm Tue–Sun* • *Adm charge*

7 Ermida de Santo Amaro

The architectural and artistic appeal of this small hilltop chapel is much greater than its rather few tourist visitors would suggest. And there's a good view. It was built in the mid-16th century to an unusual, seven-sided plan, survived the 1755 earthquake and is decorated with 16th-, 17th- and 18th-century tile panels. They show the miracles of Santo Amaro, patron saint of those who suffer fractured limbs, as well as the legend about the original chapel's founders: Galician seamen who had been shipwrecked at the mouth of the Tejo. ✆ *Calçada de Santo Amaro* • *Map C5* • *Knock on door or ask nearby if closed* • *Free*

8 Aqueduto das Águas Livres

Lisbon's long-legged aqueduct was built just over a decade before the 1755 earthquake – which it survived, continuing to supply water to the shattered city. Some facts and figures: the 35 arches marching across the Alcântara valley are up to 64 m

Museu da Marioneta

Note that young children may find some of the puppets at the Museu da Marioneta frightening.

Aqueduto das Águas Livres

(210 ft) high, making them the tallest stone arches in the world at the time they were built; the aqueduct's span is nearly 1 km (half a mile); the main water source was 58 km (36 miles) of ducting away; the system was only taken out of service in 1967. The Museu da Água organizes walks across the aqueduct.
◈ Map E2–D2 • 218 100 215

Monsanto
Monsanto is the big green bit on the maps; Lisbon's largest wooded area and its highest hill. Encroached on by construction, bisected by a motorway and blighted by prostitution and other criminality, this is still the best place to go near central Lisbon for the smell of pine trees, a fresh breeze and a walk with soil underfoot. There are a number of fenced-off recreational areas, including children's parks (see p50), tennis courts, a shooting range, a campsite and a rugby pitch. It's an area well worth exploring – in daylight. ◈ Map D2

Belém
Now part of a larger city, rather than the distant suburb it was in the pre-motorized era, Lisbon's westernmost district nonetheless retains pleasant contrasts with the city centre. Refreshing river breezes and a cluster of some of Lisbon's main sights contribute to its appeal (see pp84–5).

A Walk through West Lisbon

Morning

Begin by catching the 28 tram to its terminus at **Prazeres**. Visit the cemetery of the same name, if cemeteries are of interest, then stroll along Rua Saraiva de Carvalho past the large **Santo Condestável** church (with its attractive stained-glass windows). Drop into **Campo de Ourique** market (see p40) and pick up some fresh fruit, or just whet your appetite for lunch. Then head right along Rua Coelho da Rocha and visit **Casa Fernando Pessoa**. Lunch here, or at the cosy **Tasquinha d'Adelaide** (see p89), in Rua do Patrocínio.

Afternoon

After lunch, walk all the way down Rua Coelho da Rocha, turn right into Rua da Estrela, and proceed downhill to one of the corner entrances of **Jardim da Estrela**, where you can absorb the mid-city peace of the park. When you're ready, head for the main entrance of the park and you'll see the **Basílica de Estrela** across the square. After a visit, make your way slowly through Lapa via Rua João de Deus, which enters it on the left of the basilica. Follow the tram tracks round and then down Rua de São Domingos – veer off to left or right for extended Lapa views. Return to Rua de São Domingos and continue down it until you reach steps (there's a tile-making factory here, with a shop), which will take you down to Rua das Janelas Verdes and the **Museu de Arte Antiga** (see pp14–15).

Check out http://museudaagua.epal.pt for more information on walks across the aqueduct.

Left **Museu da Marinha (front façade)** Right **Padrão dos Descobrimentos (eastern face)**

Belém: Sights

Mosteiro dos Jerónimos
Portugal's greatest national monument is emblematic of the country's Manueline style. Dom Manuel I built the monastery and abbey in the early 16th century, in thanks for Portugal's voyages of maritime discovery (see pp10–11).

Museu de Arqueologia
Housed in the west wing of the Mosteiro dos Jerónimos, this museum exhibits archaeological finds from the Iron Age onwards. ⊗ Praça do Império • Map A6 • 213 620 000 • Open 10am–6pm Tue–Sun • Adm charge (free until 2pm Sun & public hols)

Museu da Marinha
The naval museum in the west wing of the Mosteiro dos Jerónimos covers shipbuilding and navigation. ⊗ Praça do Império • Map A6 • 213 620 019 • Open 10am–5pm (6pm in summer) Tue–Sun • Adm charge (free until 2pm Sun & public hols)

Torre de Belém
For many, this defensive tower is the masterpiece of the Manueline style. When built in 1515–20, it was almost mid-stream in the Tejo; land on the right bank was later reclaimed (see pp18–19).

Palácio de Belém
This 16th-century palace, much altered by Dom João V in the 18th century, is the working residence of Portugal's president. ⊗ Praça Afonso de Albuquerque • Map A6 • 213 614 600 • Open 10am–5pm Sat (guided visit) • Adm charge

Museu dos Coches
Lisbon's popular museum of historic coaches is housed in the former riding school of the Palácio de Belém (see p34).

Museu Colecção Berardo Arte Moderna e Contemporânea
This prestigious collection of modern and contemporary art includes works by Picasso, Andy Warhol and Jeff Koons (see p34).

Padrão dos Descobrimentos
Created in 1960 for the 500th anniversary of the death of Henry the Navigator, this monument is in the form of the prow of a ship. Don't miss the multimedia show, the Lisbon Experience. ⊗ Avenida de Brasília • Map B6 • 213 031 950 • Open May–Sep: 10am–7pm daily; Oct–Apr: 10am–6pm Tue–Sun • Adm charge

Jardim Museu Agrícola Tropical
This garden of tropical trees and plants – the research centre of the Institute for Tropical Sciences – is an oasis in the tourist bustle of Belém. ⊗ Largo dos Jerónimos • Map B5–6 • 213 637 023 • Open 9am–6pm Mon–Fri (5pm in winter), 11am–7pm Sat–Sun (10am–5pm in winter) • Adm charge

Palácio da Ajuda
The Neo-Classical palace in Ajuda was left unfinished in 1807 when the royal family was forced into exile in Brazil. ⊗ Calçada da Ajuda • Map B5 • 213 637 095 • Open 10am–5:30pm Thu–Tue • Adm charge

Price Categories

For a three course meal for one with half a bottle of wine (or equivalent meal), taxes and extra charges.

€	under €15
€€	€15–€20
€€€	€20–€30
€€€€	€30–€40
€€€€€	over €40

Vela Latina

🔟 Belém: Restaurants

1 Belém Bar Café
This large bar, restaurant and nightclub affords views through a glass wall to the riverside. The Mediterranean-style food pleases a fairly sharp crowd. ◈ *Avenida de Brasília, Pavilhão Poente • Map C6 • 213 624 232 • Closed Sun & Mon • €€€€*

2 Solar do Embaixador
Tasty Brazilian specialities share the menu with more traditional Portuguese fare at this jolly eatery in a Belém backstreet. ◈ *Rua do Embaizador 210 • Map B6 • 213 625 111 • €€*

3 Vela Latina
Overlooking the Doca do Bom Sucesso near the Torre de Belém, this pleasant restaurant with a terrace specializes in creatively prepared fish and seafood. Meat dishes include quail in raspberry sauce. ◈ *Doca do Bom Sucesso • Map A6 • 213 017 118 • Closed Sun • €€€€*

4 Nosolo Itália
Fine river views and a wide choice (even for vegetarians) of pastas, pizzas and salads are on offer here. ◈ *Avenida de Brasília 202 • Map B6 • 213 015 969 • €€€*

5 Enoteca de Belém
This delightful little wine bar has an outstanding range of Portuguese wines as well as a delicious selection of tapas-style tasting plates. ◈ *Travessa de Marta Pinto 10–12 • Map B6 • 213 631 511 • Closed Mon • €€€*

6 Cais de Belém
Next to the Jardim de Belém, the traditional Cais de Belém does a reliable *arroz de peixe com gambas* (fish rice with prawns). ◈ *Rua Vieira Portuense 64 • Map B6 • 213 621 537 • Closed Tue D; Wed • €€€*

7 Picanha de Belém
This lively place specializes in flavourful *picanha*, a Brazilian cut of rump steak, grilled and served with stewed black beans, rice, baked potatoes and salad. For non-carnivores there's grilled fillet of grouper. ◈ *Rua Vieira Portuense 78 • Map B6 • 213 658 300 • €€€*

8 Estufa Real
Set in former greenhouses in Ajuda's botanical garden, this restaurant serves Portuguese fare. Sunday brunch is popular. ◈ *Calçada do Galvão (Jardim Botânico da Ajuda) • Map B5 • 213 619 400 • Closed D; Sat • €€€*

9 In Rio Lounge
With a popular terrace, a retro-groovy bar and a slightly more formal restaurant, this low building on the riverside is busy all day. Grilled fish and seafood dominate the menu. ◈ *Avenida de Brasília, Pavilhão Nascente 311 • Map C6 • 213 626 248 • €€€*

10 Os Jerónimos
This simple bar-restaurant provides a serious take on traditional Portuguese food. Portions are large. ◈ *Rua de Belém 74 • Map B6 • 213 638 423 • Closed Sat • €€€*

Left **West Lisbon waterfront, with Ponte 25 de Abril and Cristo Rei** Right **Jardim Botânico da Ajuda**

West Lisbon: Best of the Rest

1 Antiga Confeitaria de Belém
This celebrated café and pastry shop is the originator of *pastéis de Belém* – custard tarts known as *pastéis de nata* elsewhere. Ⓝ *Rua de Belém 84–92 • Map B6*

2 Coisas do Arco do Vinho
Within the CCB, one of the best wine shops in Lisbon excels with its quality Portuguese wines from smaller producers. Ⓝ *Rua Bartolomeu Dias, units 7–8 • Map A6*

3 Centro Cultural de Belém
Controversial when it opened in 1992, this starkly modern fortress of culture is well regarded for its broad programming and the relevance of its exhibitions. The CCB hosts the latest talent in dance, opera, theatre, music and film. Ⓝ *Praça do Império • Map A6 • 213 612 400 • Open 10am–7pm Mon–Sun • Free • www.ccb.pt*

4 Fundação Museu Arpad Szenes-Vieira da Silva
Housed in a former silk factory, this museum is dedicated to the work of Portuguese Modernist painter Maria Helena Vieira da Silva and her Hungarian husband, Arpad Szenes *(see p35)*.

5 Waterfront to Belém
A family favourite for Sunday strolling and biking, the riverside promenade runs almost uninterrupted from the Docas area to the Torre de Belém *(see pp18–19)*. Ⓝ *Avenida de Brasília • Map C6*

6 Jardim Botânico da Ajuda
Portugal's oldest botanical garden, was laid out in 1768. It has a vast 400-year-old Madeiran dragon tree and box hedges. The Estufa Real *(see p85)* serves lunch. Ⓝ *Calçada da Ajuda • Map B5 • 213 622 503 • Open 9am–8pm daily (7pm in Apr, 6pm Oct–Mar) • Adm charge*

7 Lapa streets
Stroll past Lapa's many grand residences and humbler homes for an essential Lisbon contrast, and exhilarating topography. Ⓝ *Rua de São Caetano, Rua do Sacramento, Rua de São Félix • Map E4–5*

8 Docas area
Overlooking the Santo Amaro marina, this waterfront row of converted warehouses is one of Lisbon's most buzzing bar, restaurant and nightlife areas. Ⓝ *Doca de Santo Amaro • Map D5*

9 Miradouro de Santa Catarina
This central Lisbon viewing point overlooking the river is a popular place to meet for a beer or a coffee. Thankfully, few visitors seem much awed by the hirsute and hollow-eyed statue of Adamastor *(see p36)*.

10 Igreja da Memória
This Neo-Classical church was built in 1760 in thanks for the narrow escape Dom José I had from an assassination attempt. Ⓝ *Calçada do Galvão • Map B5 • Open for mass: 6pm Mon–Sat, 10am Sun • Free*

Price Categories

For a three course meal for one with half a bottle of wine (or equivalent meal), taxes and extra charges.

€ under €15
€€ €15–€20
€€€ €20–€30
€€€€ €30–€40
€€€€€ over €40

Água no Bico

🔟 Gay Lisbon

1 Frágil
Popular club owned by musician and composer Rodrigo Leão, with an underlying theme that stretches back to the 1980s. The crowd is a mix of gay men, lesbians and a scattering of heterosexuals. ✎ Rua da Atalaia 126 • Map K4

2 Sertório Sauna Club
One of Lisbon's newer saunas offers facilities that include Jacuzzis, a Turkish bath, saunas and a bar. ✎ Calçada da Patriarcal 38 • Map F4

3 Labyrinto
Not for the faint-hearted, this club, located close to the Portuguese parliament building, is one of the most popular spots in the city for cruising. Dress codes often border on the bizarre, but are taken very seriously.
✎ Rua dos Industriais 19 • Map F4

4 Trumps
A classic of Lisbon's gay scene, this mixed club has several bar areas, a dance floor and a snooker room, spread over two levels. ✎ Rua da Imprensa Nacional 104B • Map F4

5 Água no Bico
This gay bar attracts a crowd that is mixed in terms of age. Those wishing to surf the web can take advantage of Internet access. You'll need to ring the doorbell to get in. ✎ Rua de São Marçal 170 • Map F4

6 Finalmente
Another fixture of the Lisbon gay scene, Finalmente has a tiny dance floor and notorious drag shows. It gets going late – but when it does, it really does.
✎ Rua da Palmeira 38 • Map F4

7 Bric-a-Bar
This long-established and fairly spacious gay bar is a cruising spot. There is a choice of bars as well as a dance floor.
✎ Rua Cecílio de Sousa 82–4 • Map F4

8 Memorial
Although nominally a lesbian club, this place has a fairly mixed clientele. Entertainment comes in the form of regular transvestite and comedy shows. There is a small dance floor. ✎ Rua Gustavo Matos Sequeira 42A • Map F4

9 Bar 106
This self-styled international gay bar has a club feel with games, competitions and regular party nights. With cheap draught beer (cheaper on Wednesdays), it is also one of the most affordable drinking holes in town.
✎ Rua de São Marçal 106 • Map F4

10 SS Bar
This relaxed mixed bar has a friendly atmosphere and doesn't feel like a cruising joint. Like most gay bars, it's a late starter. There are transvestite shows on Fridays and Saturdays. Ring the doorbell to enter. ✎ Calçada da Patriarcal 38 • Map F4

Left **Eclectic decor at Paródia** Right **Incógnito**

🔟 Nightlife

1 Estado Líquido
One of the seminal clubs in the Santos area has a relaxed DJ vibe and live music at weekends. A hip sushi bar opens till late up-stairs. ⊗ *Largo de Santos 5A • Map F4*

2 Foxtrot
With a rambling series of rooms, a courtyard, pool tables and kitschy decor, this old-style bar has become a quintessential Lisbon milieu. ⊗ *Travessa de Santa Teresa 28 • Map F4*

3 Incógnito
The name and door bell might suggest otherwise, but this is one of Lisbon's best venues for dancing the night away. The 80s nostalgia has been a constant; now it's mixed with newer sounds (see p42).

4 Paradise Garage
Check out this ex-warehouse venue for dance nights and occasional live music, often from bands outside the mainstream. The weekend after-hours sessions are legendary (see p42).

5 Indochina
Indochina is one of a quartet of purpose-converted warehouse clubs in the riverfront area between Santos and Alcântara. It is retro-modern in style, with a bar and restaurant, and has a calmer atmosphere than some of its competitors. ⊗ *Rua da Cintura do Porto de Lisboa, Armazém F • Map D5*

6 Kremlin
This classic Lisbon dance-music venue is still throbbing to the sound of house. Nearby Kapital and Konvento have the same owners, if somewhat different crowds – but at dawn all converge on Kremlin, arriving through internal passageways (see p42).

7 Speakeasy
This easy-going live music venue and somewhat overpriced restaurant is found down at the docks. Jazz, blues and funk are its specialities, with Monday night jam sessions. ⊗ *Cais das Oficinas, Armazém 115 • Map D5*

8 Alcântara-Mar
Lisbon's legendary Alcântara-Mar club is living up to most of the high expectations placed on it. Expect serious drinking, flaunting and dancing to house and techno until well into the early hours (see p42).

9 Paródia
Dating from the mid-1970s, this miniature bar has retained the decor of that era. If you remember the 70s, the effect is nostalgic; if you don't, it's intriguing. Ring the bell. ⊗ *Rua do Patrocínio 26B • Map E4*

10 Bar Lounge
This friendly, relaxed venue plays a mix of indie and electronic pop and rock music, with regular live music sessions (see p42).

➡ *Also on the riverfront between Alcântara and Santos, check out Blues, Dock's Club and Queen's.*

Price Categories

For a three course	€	under €15
meal for one with half	€€	€15–€20
a bottle of wine (or	€€€	€20–€30
equivalent meal), taxes	€€€€	€30–€40
and extra charges.	€€€€€	over €40

Waiters prepare for an evening at Kais

🔟 Restaurants

1 Alcântara Café
When this stunning bar and pleasantly cosmopolitan restaurant opened in the late 1980s, Lisbon had neither seen nor tasted its like. It still impresses. ⊗ *Rua Maria Luísa Holstein 15 • Map D5 • 213 637 176 • Closed L; Mon • €€€€*

2 Tromba Rija
An offshoot of a famous restaurant in Leiria, this riverside place serves Portuguese fare. ⊗ *Rua do Cintura do Porto de Lisboa, Edifício 254, Armazém I • Map E5 • 213 971 507 • Closed Sun D; Mon L • €€€€*

3 Aya Bistrôt
The Aya restaurants are often regarded as serving the city's best Japanese food. At this one, it arrives on a conveyor belt. ⊗ *Galerias Twin Towers, Rua de Campolide 351 • Map E2 • 217 271 155 • €€*

4 Kais/Adega do Kais
Housed in an awe-inspiring former engine shed, Kais offers a lightly modernized Portuguese menu. In the basement, the Adega do Kais is a traditional *rodízio*; customers are served from a selection of 20 dishes, for a fixed price. ⊗ *Rua do Cintura do Porto de Lisboa, Cais da Viscondessa • Map E5 • 213 932 931 • Closed L; Sun, Mon • €€€*

5 Terra
This lovely vegetarian restaurant serves vegetable and meat-substitute dishes, as well as sushi. ⊗ *Rua da Palmeira 15 • Map F4 • 213 421 407 • Closed Mon • €€*

6 Nariz de Vinho Tinto
This tasting restaurant has an ambitious menu of traditional Portuguese dishes. The customer is offered a select range of everything, from mineral waters to olive oils and coffees – not to mention the actual menu and wine list. ⊗ *Rua do Conde 75 • Map E5 • 213 953 035 • Closed Sat & Sun L & Mon • €€€€*

7 Clube de Jornalistas
Housed in the building of a Portuguese journalists' club, this attractive restaurant has an inner courtyard and serves top-notch modern international food. ⊗ *Rua das Trinas 129 • Map E4 • 213 977 138 • Closed Sun • €€€*

8 Tasquinha d'Adelaide
A long-time neighbourhood favourite, Adelaide specializes in the cuisine of northern Portugal. The space is small and intimate. ⊗ *Rua do Patrocínio 70–74 • Map E4 • 213 962 239 • Closed Sun • €€€*

9 O Mercado
What better place for a restaurant than in the same building as a food market? O Mercado cooks local food with verve. ⊗ *Mercado Rosa Agulhas, Rua Leão de Oliveira • Map D5 • 213 649 113 • Closed Sun D • €€*

10 A Travessa
Set in a convent building, this is one of Lisbon's most characterful restaurants in terms both of location and food (see p44).

Left **Theatre Museum, Parque do Monteiro-Mor** Right **Dolphins performing at Jardim Zoológico**

Avenida & North Lisbon

A VENIDA DA LIBERDADE EXTENDS NORTHWARDS *from Restauradores for just over a kilometre (more than half a mile), at a slight incline. It ends at the roundabout named after the Marquis of Pombal, who became Lisbon's strong man after the 1755 earthquake. He stands at the centre of the swirl of traffic, flanked by a lion, surveying the city centre he created. If you carry on up to the top of Eduardo VII park and look to your right, Lisbon's early 20th-century northern extensions (now very much a part of the "centre") stretch out before you. Closer at hand is the esteemed Gulbenkian museum; further afield, the 21st-century vistas of Parque das Nações.*

🔟 Sights

1. Rotunda Marquês de Pombal/Parque Eduardo VII
2. Museu Gulbenkian
3. Avenidas Novas
4. Campo Pequeno
5. Museu da Cidade
6. Football Stadiums
7. Parque do Monteiro-Mor
8. Palácio dos Marqueses da Fronteira
9. Jardim Zoológico
10. Parque das Nações

Nymph fountain,
Parque Eduardo VII

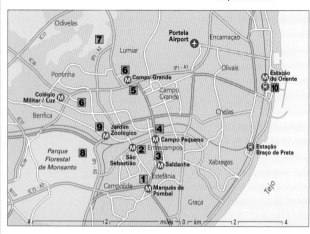

Sign up for DK's email newsletter on traveldk.com

1 Rotunda Marquês de Pombal/Parque Eduardo VII

The roundabout where Pombal and his lion pose was the northern limit of the city he conceived. The orderly park behind him was first laid out in the late 19th century, as a green extension of Avenida da Liberdade – and to replace the pedestrian Passeio Público that the Avenida had usurped. In 1903, Parque da Liberdade was renamed in honour of the visiting English King Edward VII. It is really more of a promenade – and its incline makes it a demanding one – than a park. For proper greenery, seek out the Estufa Fria and Estufa Quente greenhouses along the northwestern edge of the park. A walk to the top is rewarded with good views of central Lisbon. At the very top are the pleasant Linha d'Água café and Eleven restaurant *(see p44)*. ✆ *Map F2–3*

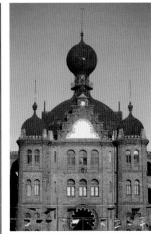

Neo-Moorish façade, Campo Pequeno

Avenida da República, and 21st-century shopping has come to Praça Duque de Saldanha, but this area of Lisbon is still a respectable residential one. ✆ *Map F1–2*

2 Museu Gulbenkian

The museum founded on the collections and fortune of Armenian exile Calouste Gulbenkian is one of Lisbon's most satisfying tourist sights *(see pp24–5)*.

3 Avenidas Novas

The "New Avenues" – now a century old – are an uneven grid of streets immediately to the north of Pombal and Parque Eduardo VII. The area is a fairly typical example of late 19th- to early 20th-century planning: wide streets have tree-lined lanes down the middle, and grand residences line the main avenues. It became the heart of a newer, upper-middle-class Lisbon, away from the crowded conditions and perceived unsalubriousness of the old riverside districts. It has been much altered along its main axis,

Lalique at Museu Gulbenkian

4 Campo Pequeno

One of Lisbon's most striking buildings, the Campo Pequeno bullring is a delightful arabic-oriental pastiche from 1892 with onion cupolas and keyhole windows. It stands on a spot where bullfights *(see p92)* have been held since at least the first half of the 18th century. The area was then part of a vast terrain of country estates a short ride from the centre. It reopened in 2006 after several years of repair and underground extension which created a modern leisure and shopping complex lit by discrete light wells. None of this is meant to intrude on the drama played out in the ring, which can also be roofed over for use as a concert or show venue. ✆ *Map F1* • *217 820 575* • *Bullfights traditionally on Thu, May–Sep* • *Adm for events varies*

Museu da Cidade

The city museum is housed in an 18th-century palace, Palácio Pimenta, at the top of Campo Grande. The palace itself is worth seeing, in particular for the kitchen's "still-life" tiles depicting animal carcasses hung to tenderize. The permanent exhibition traces Lisbon's development from the earliest settlements on the banks of the Tejo. Perhaps the most evocative display is the large three-dimensional model of Lisbon as it is believed to have looked before the earthquake in 1755. ® Campo Grande 245 • Map C1 • 217 513 200 • Open 10am–1pm, 2–6pm Tue–Sun • Adm charge (free Sun)

Tiled terrace leading to the chapel of the Palácio Fronteira

Riding Against the Bull

Portuguese bullfighting is always introduced with the qualification that the bull isn't killed. This attempt to appease opponents of bullfighting (and possibly the bulls themselves) is both misguided and disingenuous. In fact the bull is unceremoniously slaughtered after the fight – surely a rather academic distinction from the animal's perspective. The most interesting difference compared with Spanish bullfighting – once you recognize that both forms successively wound the animal in order to make the finale possible – is that a rider on an unprotected horse (the bull's horns are wrapped) performs an equestrian ballet with the bull, while sticking short spears in between its shoulder blades to make its head hang lower. The finale is then performed by a group of intrepid *forcados* on foot, who charge the bull in single file, throwing themselves between its horns and over one side in order to topple it and hold it fast.

Football Stadiums

Lisbon's two major football teams, Benfica and Sporting, both built new stadiums – on the sites of their respective old ones – for the Euro 2004 championship, held in Portugal. Sporting's Estádio José Alvalade is a green and yellow cake tin (team colours are actually green and white) on the northern city limits, not far from the airport. A short distance west along the Segunda Circular ring road, opposite the enormous Colombo shopping centre, sits Benfica's Estádio da Luz, an airier edifice reminiscent of a helix on its side; it's partly painted red, the team colour. Both stadiums also incorporate modern leisure complexes. ® Rua Fernando da Fonseca; Avenida General Norton de Matos • Map B1 • 217 516 000; 217 219 500 • Match tickets around €10

Parque do Monteiro-Mor

Despite its unpromising location next to one of the major northern exits from Lisbon, this lovely Italianate park is one of the city's best oases. With its palace – now housing two moderately interesting museums, those of Theatre and Costume – it is a reminder of what Lisbon's hinterland was once like. ® Largo Júlio de Castilho • Map B1 • 217 567 620 • Open 10am–6pm Wed–Sun, 2–6pm Tue • Adm charge (covers park and both museums)

8 Palácio dos Marqueses da Fronteira

A 17th-century former hunting pavilion, expanded after the 1755 earthquake, this manor house and its gardens are one of Lisbon's most rewarding sights. The formal gardens are full of statues and tiled panels, from busts of Portuguese kings to allegorical representations of the seasons and the zodiac. Highlights inside the palace include the Battle Room, with depictions of battles during the War of Restoration against Spain – in which the first Marquis fought. Fronteira Palace is still owned and lived in by the 12th Marquis, who collects contemporary art and sometimes stages exhibitions. ⊗ *Largo de São Domingos de Benfica 1 • Map B2 • 217 782 023 • Guided tours Mon–Sat (Jun–Sep: 10:30am, 11am, 11:30am, noon; Oct–May: 11am, noon) • Adm charge*

9 Jardim Zoológico

Lisbon's Zoo is a sprightly centenarian, incorporating a small amusement park and the usual incarcerated beasts *(see p50)*.

10 Parque das Nações

The former Expo 98 site is now a business and leisure area, with exhibition spaces, events venues and a variety of sights *(see pp16–17)*.

Knowledge Pavilion, Parque das Nações

To the Gulbenkian and Beyond

Morning

🕐 Begin at the **Pombal roundabout**. An underpass leads to the statue, where you can study its various representations of tidal waves and destruction, as well as of the enlightened despot's many reforms. Cross back to the bottom of **Parque Eduardo VII** and set out for the summit; in summertime it's best not to leave it too late in the morning, as the walk is unshaded and it gets hot early. If you need a break, dive into the cool of the **Estufa Fria** and **Quente greenhouses**. At the top, ponder the symbolism of João Cutileiro's **Monument to 25 April** – not one of his most communicative works – and its contrast with Keil do Amaral's **twin columns**. Then climb the last bit of the hill to **Linha d'Água**; lunch here, or at the adjacent **Eleven**, whose Michelin star is deserved.

Afternoon

After lunch, continue past **El Corte Inglés** and on to the side entrance of the **Gulbenkian Museum**, at the north end of Avenida António Augusto de Aguiar. Expect to spend most of the afternoon in the museum – or else give it a quick browse and decide what to come back for. Stroll through the park and exit it on Rua Marquês de Sá Bandeira, then take Rua Miguel Bombarda for a taste of the **Avenidas Novas**. Turn left on to Avda da República and walk a few blocks north to **Campo Pequeno** and its Neo-Moorish bullring. Even if you disapprove of bull-fighting you can enjoy a drink in the park surrounding the whimsical arena.

Left **Jazz at Hot Clube** Right **Centro Colombo shopping centre**

Best of the Rest

1 Hot Clube
Lisbon's oldest jazz club seems always to have been here, indifferent to shifting fashions. It is the kind of small basement club where the gap between artists and audience evaporates. ⌾ *Praça da Alegria 48 • Map K1*

2 Avenida Designer Shops
The former Passeio Público (Public Promenade) still hasn't recovered from the introduction of vehicles over a century ago. However, the appearance of inter-national designer shops attests that Lisbon's main avenue has regained some of its pedigree. ⌾ *Avenida da Liberdade • Map F3*

3 El Corte Inglés
The Spanish chain has one of its largest complexes in Lisbon, including the city's only true department store – plus restaurants, cinemas and luxury apartments. ⌾ *Avenida António Augusto de Aguiar • Map F2*

4 Parque da Bela Vista
A large urban park, Bela Vista hosts the Rock in Rio fest-ival, which takes place every two years (next one will be in 2012). ⌾ *Avenida Gago Coutinho*

5 Maxime
Formerly a grand cabaret venue, then a strip joint, Maxime has reinvented itself as a stage for a rich variety of comedy and musical performances. ⌾ *Praça da Alegria 58 • Map K1*

6 Culturgest
Housed in the vast post-modern headquarters of a state-owned bank, Culturgest stages music, dance, theatre and exhibitions *(see p35).*

7 Benfica
This northwestern suburb of Lisbon, now very much a part of the city, has its own rhythm. The famous football team did not start up here – it moved in – but this is still one of Lisbon's proudest *bairros.* ⌾ *Estrada de Benfica • Map B2*

8 Alameda
In a part of the city where tourists rarely venture, Alameda's narrow common and its Mussolini-esque lighted fountain provide a sense of Lisbon as it was before 1974. ⌾ *Alameda Dom Afonso Henriques, Avenida Almirante Reis • Map G1*

9 Centro Colombo
Described as the biggest shopping centre in the Iberian peninsula, Colombo has a stag-gering 420 shops, 60 restaurants and 10 cinemas. ⌾ *Avenida Lusiada • Map B2 • 10am–midnight daily*

10 Museu Rafael Bordalo Pinheiro
This museum dedicated to Portugal's best-known caricaturist, political lampoonist and ceramic artist offers a thorough but light-hearted look at Portugal's history and temperament. ⌾ *Campo Grande 382 • Map C1 • 217 550 468 • Open 10am–6pm Tue–Sun • Adm charge*

Price Categories

For a three course meal for one with half a bottle of wine (or equivalent meal), taxes and extra charges.	
€	under €15
€€	€15–€20
€€€	€20–€30
€€€€	€30–€40
€€€€€	over €40

Enoteca

🔟 Restaurants and Cafés

1 Fusion
This international fusion and sushi restaurant and bar serves dishes using fresh market products. The kitchen has glass walls through which you can observe the talented chefs. ⊗ *Rua de Santa Marta 35 • Map F3 • 213 150 212 • Closed Sun • €€€*

2 Eleven
Lisbon's premier gourmet restaurant, with soft lighting and huge windows overlooking the city, is found at the top of Parque Eduardo VII *(see p37)*. Modern Mediterranean food by Joachim Koerper has earned it a Michelin star *(see p44)*.

3 Ribadouro
This is one of the city's best *cervejarias* (beer halls). Like many, it specializes in seafood, some of it pricey. ⊗ *Rua do Salitre 2–12 • Map K1 • 213 549 411 • €€*

4 Enoteca
The city's most appealing wine bar serves tasty small dishes to go with its wide choice of wines. ⊗ *Rua da Mãe d'Água • Map J2 • 213 422 079 • Closed L; Mon • €€€*

5 Psi
This vegetarian restaurant offers dishes from around the world in a garden setting – and a spiritual vibe. The Dalai Lama dropped by on a visit to Lisbon. ⊗ *Alameda Santo António dos Capuchos, Jardim dos Sabores • Map G3 • 213 590 573 • Closed Sun • €*

6 Assuka
One of Lisbon's best-value Japanese restaurants offers great sushi and friendly service. ⊗ *Rua de São Sebastião 150 • Map F2 • 213 149 345 • Closed Sun L • €€*

7 Café Mexicana
This busy café and restaurant in the Guerra Junqueiro/Roma shopping area provides a neat slice of middle-class Lisbon life, along with coffee and ample pastries. The 1960s interior has a certain something. ⊗ *Avenida Guerra Junqueiro 30 • Map G1*

8 Magnolia Caffé
Lisbon has several branches of this modern, ambitious café chain. This, like the others, combines tasteful surroundings with fresh bakery products, salads, fruit juices and serious coffee. ⊗ *Campo Pequeno 2A • Map C2*

9 Jardim do Torel
Come to this café, set in the 19th-century Jardim do Torel, for light snacks or an apéritif on the terrace, which affords a sweeping mid-town panorama. Prices are steeper than average but the location is priceless. ⊗ *Jardim do Torel • Map L1*

10 Pastelaria Versailles
Wonderful if slightly yellowed, this café and pastry shop has a grandiose interior, harassed brylcreemed waiters and worldly-wise elderly lady customers. ⊗ *Avenida República 15A • Map F1*

Left **Casino Estoril** Right **Cascais Marina**

Lisbon Coast

ITS RIVIERA-RIVALLING HEYDAY MAY BE A DISTANT MEMORY NOW, *but the varied coastline from the mouth of the Tejo to Europe's westernmost point has newer attractions too. Known locally as the linha, the coastal region has become one of Lisbon's most populous suburban zones – and yet it retains a laid-back holiday atmosphere. Above and behind it, Sintra's rock-strewn slopes and fragrant woods have a much more ancient ambience.*

View from Cabo da Roca

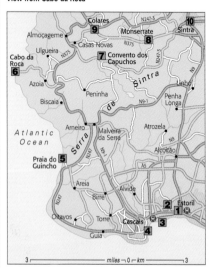

Sights

1. Estoril Casino
2. Monte Estoril
3. Cascais–Estoril Waterfront
4. Cascais Marina
5. Guincho
6. Cabo da Roca
7. Convento dos Capuchos
8. Monserrate
9. Colares
10. Sintra

Preceding pages **Palácio da Pena, rising above the wooded Parque da Pena, Sintra**

Cascais–Estoril waterfront

Estoril Casino
Large and rather loud in style, the entertainment heart of Estoril is more than just "Europe's biggest casino", with both gaming tables and slot machines. It has several good restaurants, an art gallery, a varied concert calendar, a glitzy disco, a theatre stage and titillating floor shows. The palm-lined park in front adds a welcome touch of old-world glamour. ⊗ *Avenida Dr Stanley Ho • 214 667 700 • Open 3pm–3am daily • Adm varies • www.casino-estoril.pt*

Monte Estoril
The ridge that separates Estoril from Cascais was the site of the earliest resort development, during the first half of the 20th century. It is now a captivating jumble of grand mansions, shopping arcades and apartment hotels – and still manages to be leafy and quiet in parts. Its railway station is reached by way of a tunnel under the busy *Marginal* coast road.

Cascais–Estoril Waterfront
Estoril and Cascais are linked by a promenade which runs just above the beach, but mostly out of sight of the coast road. By far the best walk in either resort, it is lined with small restaurants and bars and occasionally sprayed by Atlantic breakers.

Cascais Marina
Just beyond the centre of the town, and curving around the original fortress on the headland, Cascais Marina has 650 berths and can accommodate yachts up to 36 m (118 ft) long, with a maximum draught of 6 m (20 ft). The many small shops and restaurants also attract a non-sailing crowd. Nearby are the large municipal park of Cascais, the Condes de Castro Guimarães Museum and the Coconuts nightclub *(see p102)*. ⊗ *Casa de São Bernardo • 214 824 857 • Reception open 9am–7pm (6pm in winter) • www.marinacascais.pt*

Guincho
Still relatively undeveloped, the windswept coastline beyond Cascais, extending to Cabo da Roca, is exhilarating and scenic, particularly at Guincho. The beach of the same name is popular for surfing (although it's not recommended for beginners), and the broad sands are good for other beach sports as well as for brisk walks. When it's too windy to swim or sunbathe here, there are several smaller, more protected beaches on either side. Some of the best restaurants in the area lie along the Guincho road *(see p103)*.

Guincho

Convento dos Capuchos

Cabo da Roca

The westernmost point of mainland Europe is a suitably dramatic clifftop location marked by a lighthouse. There is also a quotation from Luís de Camões' epic poem *The Lusiads*, carved in stone. But beware: Cape Roca is subject to the climatic peculiarities of the whole Sintra region. Take a jumper, even if it's hot when you leave Cascais; temperatures can be 10 degrees lower here, and the winds strong. Collectors of memorabilia can buy a certificate to prove that they have walked on the continent's western extremity. There is a good café and restaurant, called O Moinho, near the turnoff from the Sintra road, and Ursa beach *(see p49)* lies just north of the point.

Convento dos Capuchos

Standing above Cabo da Roca, near Peninha *(see p102)*, this 16th-century Franciscan monastery is a striking example of monastic frugality, and thus a rarity among Portugal's generally opulent religious buildings. The Capuchin monks' cells are small and plain, hewn from rock and lined with cork against echoes and the cold. The minimal decoration is limited to communal areas such as the chapel, the refectory and the chapterhouse. The small fountain could almost be in a Buddhist forest retreat.
◈ *On road N247-3 • Open 9:30am–6pm daily (8pm in summer) • Adm charge*

Monserrate

These lovely gardens, with their blend of natural and artificial elements, the exotic and the familiar, epitomize some of the essential characteristics of the Sintra region and its inhabitants. Just look at the artificial "ruin" in the lower garden – it might have been designed for Walt Disney's

Colares Wine

Once famous for its velvety, long-lived red wines made from the Ramisco grape – one of Europe's few survivors of the phylloxera plague – Colares seems now to be reduced to wine history. Wine is still made, but very little has any of the qualities associated with classic Colares. It seems that the costs of maintaining the old vines – and of planting new ones deep in the sand that protected them from the scourge of the vine louse – is too high.

Sign up for DK's email newsletter on traveldk.com

The Jungle Book – or at the rolling lawns flanked by tropical trees, or the marvellous pastiche of the palace-pavilion *(see p27)*.

9 Colares

This pretty, peaceful village between Sintra and the sea gave its name to one of Portugal's most famous table wines, now made in only tiny amounts of variable quality. (Wine-lovers can visit the cooperative in Colares, at the beginning of the road to Praia das Maçãs, or go out to Azenhas do Mar and look up Paulo Bernardino da Costa, a stubborn producer.) All the same, it's well worth lingering in the older parts of Colares, shaded by plane trees with their peeling, mottled bark. Seek out the restaurant and tea salon Colares Velho in the church square, and soak up the old atmosphere of privilege edged by penury.

10 Sintra

To have seen the world and left out Sintra is not truly to have seen – thus goes, more or less, a Spanish saying. When you visit this ravishing hill-town, set on the northern slopes of the Serra, it's easy to understand why it was the preferred summer retreat of Portuguese kings *(see pp26–7)*.

Fonte Mourisca, Sintra

A Sintra Drive

Morning

Starting out from **Cascais**, drive along the Guincho coast towards Cabo da Roca (road N247). After Guincho beach, the road begins to climb. Follow the main road past the turning to Malveira da Serra. Turn off to the left for **Cabo da Roca** or, a tiny bit farther on, to the right for **Peninha** and **Convento dos Capuchos**. The latter choice offers opportunities for walks in the woods and views across the Serra; the former an invigorating lungful of sea air and the possibility of a drink at the **O Moinho** bar. Back on the main road, carry on towards **Colares** and stop there for lunch, taking the time to explore the village.

Afternoon

From Colares take the smaller road (N375 heading inland) towards Sintra, which will lead you past Eugaria and to **Monserrate**. Make an extended stop at Monserrate, giving yourself time to enjoy the gardens. The area above the parking lot outside the entrance is a popular picnic spot. Carry on along the lovely road that tunnels through the woods until you reach stately **Seteais**, where tea might be in order. A short distance further on you will come to **Quinta da Regaleira** – worth visiting for its gardens and esoterica – before you enter **Sintra** proper. Follow the road up, until you find parking above the main town, then walk down and do the sights or head straight to **Lawrence's** *(see p116)* for dinner. You can return to Cascais (and Lisbon) via the faster N9.

Left **Palácio and Parque da Pena** Right **Boca do Inferno**

🔟 Best of the Rest

1 Azenhas do Mar
Small houses huddle together in this cliff-top village that spills down towards a rock pool by the Atlantic ocean. With several restaurants, it is popular for Sunday lunch outings. ✆ N375

2 Parque da Pena
The paths in the park around the Palácio da Pena lead to the highest point in the Sintra hills – Cruz Alta, at 530 m (1,740 ft). ✆ N247-3 • Open 9:30am–6pm (8pm in summer) daily • Adm charge

3 Peninha
The small Capela de Nossa Senhora de Penha was built at the turn of the 17th century. In 1918 António Carvalho Monteiro, the millionaire owner of the Quinta da Regaleira (see p27), added a mock-fortified eagle's nest residence. ✆ N247

4 Museu Condes de Castro Guimarães
This tower and grand villa on a small creek just beyond Cascais marina (see p99) are said to have been inspired by a painting.
✆ Avenida Rei Humberto II de Itália • 214 825 401 • Open 10am–5pm Tue–Sun • Adm charge

5 Fábrica da Pólvora
A gunpowder factory back in the 15th century, this is now a cultural and leisure centre.
✆ Estrada das Fontaínhas, Barcarena • 214 381 400 • Open 9am–5pm (6pm in summer) daily • Adm charge varies

6 Boca do Inferno
The rocky coastline beyond Cascais is full of crevices cut by the waves. The Mouth of Hell is a particularly deep one, where the waves roar in and then shoot up a vertical hole, creating a geyser-like jet of spray. ✆ Estrada da Boca do Inferno (N247-8)

7 Coconuts
Cascais' best-known disco, aka the Nuts Club, is located right on the rocky coastline, next to the Santa Maria lighthouse. There are indoor and outdoor bars and dance floors. ✆ Avenida Rei Humberto de Itália 7

8 Cascais Cultural Centre
Opened in 2000, after lengthy renovation of a 17th-century convent building, this cultural centre holds regular exhibitions and concerts. ✆ Avenida Rei Humberto II de Itália • 214 848 900 • Open 10am–6pm Tue–Sun • Adm charge varies

9 Golf courses
There are eight golf courses along the Lisbon coast. Most are good, but Penha Longa, between Cascais and Sintra, and Oitavos, in the Quinta da Marinha complex, stand out.

10 Autódromo do Estoril
The Formula One Portuguese Grand Prix was held at the Estoril racetrack between 1984 and 1996. Today it hosts MotoGP and A1 Grand Prix events, among others. ✆ N9, Alcabideche

➡ *For more on Sintra* **See pp26–7**

Price Categories

For a three course meal for one with half a bottle of wine (or equivalent meal), taxes and extra charges.

€	under €15
€€	€15–€20
€€€	€20–€30
€€€€	€30–€40
€€€€€	over €40

Verbasco

🔟 Restaurants

1 Porto de Santa Maria
Occupying a low, modern building, overlooking the dramatic coastline near Guincho beach, is one of the country's top fish and seafood restaurants. ◈ *Estrada do Guincho • 214 879 450 • Closed Mon • €€€€€*

2 Estoril Mandarim
Part of the Casino complex in Estoril, Portugal's most luxurious Chinese restaurant is also its best. ◈ *Casino do Estoril • 214 667 270 • Closed Mon, Tue • €€€€*

3 Sawasdee, Cascais
One of two Thai restaurants in Cascais, this place is centrally located. It serves all the most popular dishes as well as performances of Thai dance and song. ◈ *Beco Esconso 11, Cascais • 919 888 484 • Open Tue–Sun D only • €€€*

4 Dom Grelhas, Cascais
Located in Casa da Guia, a gated, cliff-side collection of restaurants and small shops, Dom Grelhas specializes in grilled meat and fish. Meals are accompanied by wide views of the sea. ◈ *Casa da Guia, Estrada do Guincho • 214 839 967 • €€€*

5 Fortaleza do Guincho
Magnificently sited in a 17th-century fortress on the Guincho coast, this is a fine restaurant with a modern French menu that makes good use of Portuguese ingredients. ◈ *Estrada do Guincho • 214 870 491 • €€€€€*

6 O Pereira, Cascais
This small, friendly restaurant serves hearty Portuguese food, prepared in a timeless way. ◈ *Travessa da Bela Vista 92, Cascais • 214 831 215 • Closed Thu • €€*

7 Verbasco, Cascais
Sophisticated modern cuisine is served here in the airy club-house of the Oitavos golf course at Quinta da Marinha. ◈ *Quinta da Marinha Oitavos Golf • 214 860 606 • Open L only • €€€€€*

8 Four Seasons Grill, Estoril
This is one of the Lisbon coast's most sophisticated fine-dining venues. Set on a stylish mezzanine and lower floor, it changes its menu and decor according to the seasons. ◈ *Hotel Palácio Estoril, Rua Particular • 214 680 400 • Open D only • €€€€€*

9 Bar das Avencas
Seemingly hanging off the cliff above a quiet beach, this simple but well-designed bar serves sandwiches, salads and hamburgers, as well as a couple of other unfussy cooked dishes. ◈ *Avenida Marginal (Parede) • 214 572 717 • Closed Tue in winter • €*

10 Aromi, Cascais
Located on the main pedestrianized street in the old part of Cascais, Aromi specializes in fine, home-made Italian cuisine. House favourites include fresh swordfish and tuna. ◈ *Rua Frederico Arouca • 214 862 191 • €€€*

Both Porto de Santa Maria and Fortaleza do Guincho have one Michelin star.

STREETSMART

Getting to &
Around Lisbon
106

General Information
107

Health & Security
108

Banking &
Communications
109

Eating, Lodging &
Shopping Tips
110

Things to Avoid
111

Places to Stay
112–117

LISBON'S TOP 10

Left **Tourist tram** Centre **Metro sign** Right **Lisbon taxi**

Getting to and around Lisbon

1 Airport
Lisbon's Portela airport has two terminals – one for domestic flights only. Transfers to the centre, 7 km (4 miles) away, cost €15–18 by taxi. Allow 20–30 minutes, or twice that during the rush hour.

2 Railway Stations
Santa Apolónia station is the terminus for the high-speed Alfa Pendular service and for trains from Madrid and the north of Portugal. Most trains from the south and east (except the local Fertagus trains) arrive at Barreiro on the Tejo, from where a ferry makes the crossing to Terreiro do Paço.

3 Arriving by Road
From the south and east, drivers arrive on the A2 motorway. The A12 branches off the A2 just after Setúbal and leads to the 17-km (11-mile) Vasco da Gama bridge, which is the best approach for the north and east of the city. For the centre and west, you should stay on the A2 and cross on the 25 de Abril suspension bridge. Arrival from the north is on the A1.

4 Trams and Funiculars
Trams and funiculars are Lisbon's most appealing forms of public transport, but not its most efficient. The most useful trams for seeing the city are the 28 and the 25. The 15 runs on a modern, fast line from Praça da Figueira to Belém and Algés. Funiculars carry weary *lisboetas* up three of the city's hills.

5 Metro and Buses
Covering most of the city except the west, the metro is the fastest way of getting around. Trains run from 6:30am to 1am. Tickets for buses are the same as for trams and funiculars. They may be bought on boarding or in advance at Carris booths.

6 Ferries
The busiest crossings over the Tejo, for both cars and passengers, are at Terreiro do Paço and Cais do Sodré. Ferries leave Belém for Porto Brandão and Trafaria, which have bus services to the Caparica coast.

7 Organized Tours
The Transtejo ferry company operates a daily river cruise from Terreiro do Paço from 1st April–31st October, which leaves at 3pm and returns at around 5:30pm. Carris Lisbon tours, on open-top buses and tourist trams, depart from Praça do Comércio throughout the day. They also operate three river cruises a day from the Alcântara docks (Apr–Oct: Tue–Sun).

8 Taxis
Cream or black-and-green Lisbon taxis may be hailed, caught at ranks or ordered by phone. Fares are low for Europe. Tourist taxis are dark and unmarked except for a green "A" on the bumper. They cost more and may line up at the airport taxi rank. Tipping is common.

9 Lisbon Coast Trains
Trains to Estoril and Cascais depart from the riverside Cais do Sodré station. Some terminate at Oeiras along the way. Trains to Sintra depart from Rossio and Entrecampos stations.

10 Walking
Lisbon is a safe city best explored on foot. Some of its hills are steep and the cobbled pavements get slippery in rain.

Transport

Airport
218 413 500 • www.ana-aeroportos.pt

Buses, Trams and Funicular
www.carris.pt

Ferries
210 422 400 • www.transtejo.pt

Metro
www.metrolisboa.pt

Taxis
Autocoope: 217 932 756 • Retalis Radio Taxis: 218 119 000 • Teletáxis: 218 111 100

Trains
• General train info: 808 208 208; 351 218 545 212 calls from overseas (line open 7am–11pm) • www.cp.pt

Preceding pages **View of Praça Dom Pedro IV**

Left *Agenda Cultural* listings magazine Right **Lisboa Welcome Centre**

TOP 10 General Information

1 When to Go
Summer is, of course, high season. After August, things calm down, while the sea is as warm as it ever gets. Later autumn can be very pleasant; December to February usually brings damp and chilly weather. Early spring is one of the best times to make your visit.

2 Bookings
Book hotels well ahead for stays in June, July and August. Expect mid- to top-range hotels in central Lisbon, Cascais and Estoril to be busy all year round. You may be asked for written confirmation, with a credit card number, by fax or e-mail.

3 Visas
EU nationals with a valid passport or identity card may stay for six months before needing a residence permit. Most non-EU nationals can stay for 90 days without a visa. Regulations are subject to change, so check with a Portuguese embassy or consulate before your trip.

4 Customs
Limits on what EU citizens may import for personal use are set high, though weapons, plants and perishable foods are not permitted.

5 Travelling with Children
Lisbon may not have kneeling buses or baby-care facilities at every turn, and its pavements require all-terrain push-chairs, but most *lisboetas* have an effusive love of children. Only the very smartest restaurants frown on toddler guests, and making noise is a virtue, not a sin.

6 Lisboa Welcome Center
Lisbon's tourist office is an association with more than 400 paying members. As a result it has a corporate feel and usually offers snappy service, but its members tend to be promoted at the expense of non-members. ✆ *Praça do Comércio • Map M5 • 210 312 810 • www. visitlisboa.com*

7 Websites
Try www. visitportugal.com or www.portugaltravelguide. com for tourist advice; www.maisturismo.pt for hotel listings; www. lifecooler.com for restaurant and bar listings (though it is in Portuguese); and www.portugalvirtual.pt for general information.

8 Listings Publications
Agenda Cultural is a monthly events and listings mini-magazine in Portuguese. It covers just about everything, is generally accurate – and can be picked up for free at many hotel receptions and tourist attractions. The tourist association's monthly *Follow Me Lisboa* has the fullest coverage of events in English. The current edition can be downloaded from their website. ✆ *www. visitlisboa.com*

9 English-language Newspapers
If you want an English-language newspaper try *The Portugal News* or *Algarve Resident*, both published in the Algarve and aimed at expats, but with some useful information for visitors.

10 Public Holidays
Public holidays are frequent and include Dia de Santo António, for the city's patron saint (13 Jun).

Embassies

Australian Embassy
Avda da Liberdade 200, 2E • Map F3 • 213 101 500

Canadian Embassy
Avda da Liberdade 196–200, 3 • Map F3 • 213 164 600

Indian Embassy
R Pero da Covilhã 16 • Map A5 • 213 041 090

Irish Embassy
R da Imprensa à Estrela 1, 4 • Map E4 • 213 929 440

UK Embassy
R de São Bernardo 33 • Map E4 • 213 924 000

US Embassy
Avda das Forças Armadas • Map C2 • 217 273 300

Left **Police** Centre **Pharmacy sign** Right **Heavy Lisbon traffic**

Health and Security

Health Precautions
Visitors to Portugal do not need vaccinations or to take any other health precautions ahead of their trip. Once here, a good suntan lotion is a must, particularly if you are fair-skinned. Tap water is safe, but tastes of chlorine.

Beach Safety
Beware of currents and undertow in the sea, and don't ignore the safety flags: red – no going in the sea; yellow – no swimming; green – all clear. Nasty stings in shallow water may be from poisonous scorpion fish *(peixe-aranha)* buried in the sand. The temporary intense pain and swelling can be alleviated by applying heat to the area; alternatively seek the help of a lifeguard.

Pharmacies
Pharmacies are marked by a green cross. Pharmacy staff often dispense advice as well as medication. A closed pharmacy will have a sign in its window telling you which local one is open.

Medical Treatment
EU citizens are entitled to free or sub-sidized medical treatment if they have a European Health Insurance Card with them (the replace-ment for the E111). If you don't have the card, but pay into your country's social security system, the cost of treatment can be

claimed back later, at risk of bureaucratic hassle. Private health insurance is likely to lead to more efficient treatment.

Security
Lisbon remains a safe city by the standards of most European capitals. Visitors should be wary of pickpockets – particularly on public transport – and of leaving valuables in hired cars. More serious crime is mostly confined to certain outlying areas, but walking alone at night through districts with little nocturnal activity – such as the Baixa – is not recommended.

Police
The PSP (Polícia de Segurança Pública) has a benevolent, if slightly inefficient, image. There is a police station for tourists on Restauradores, next to the national tourist office in Palácio Foz. The GNR (National Guard) has a tougher reputation.

Traffic
Foreigners are often incensed by aggressive and dangerous Portuguese driving habits.

Women Travellers
By southern European standards, Portuguese men are not that preda-tory. However, even pairs or small groups of women may be hassled on beaches and in clubs. It is often more effective to confront the pest

loudly than to ignore him, particularly if there are other people around.

Disabled Access
Disabled people will find that the metro is the most accessible form of public transport. Lisbon is hilly and has narrow cobbled pavements with parked cars often blocking the way. Most new public buildings offer good disabled access; a lack of facilities elsewhere is often compensated for by a willingness to help.

Disabled Organizations
INR (Instituto Nacional para a Reabilitação) deals with rights of disabled people and its website has an English-language section. CNAD provides information on disabled services, while Adaptacar rents modified vehicles.

Useful Organizations

Ambulance
112 (emergency); or contact nearest hospital

CNAD
218 595 332

INR
217 929 500
• *www.inr.pt*

Police
GNR: 112 (emergency)
• *PSP: 213 421 634 (Restauradores)*
• *Tourism Police: 213 421 634*

Left **Bar area, NetCenter Café** Centre **Post office** Right **Newspaper and magazine stand**

🔟 Banking and Communications

Currency
Euros are the currency in Portugal. Coins are frequently used, even the smallest denominations. Large-value notes are quite rare and may be viewed with suspicion.

Credit Cards
Major credit cards, with the exception of American Express, are widely accepted in bigger hotels, shops, restaurants and bars.

Cash Dispensers
Known as Multibanco in Lisbon, cash dispensers are ubiquitous. Most now accept debit and credit cards from the major card companies, but transaction charges apply.

Changing Money
Banks are the easiest places to use if you want to change money and charges don't vary widely. For the less common currencies, and after banking hours, seek out one of the Forex services in Rossio or one of the city's few money-changing machines, such as the one opposite the Avenida Palace hotel *(see p112).*

Post Offices
Correios (post offices) are dotted around the city, but for buying stamps use the red, coin-operated dispensers as this will save you joining lengthy queues. First-class mail is known as *correio azul.* The main post office on

Restauradores is open at weekends; others operate 9am to 6pm on weekdays.

Telephones
There are three mobile operators: TMN (with numbers beginning 96), Vodafone (91) and Optimus (93). Coverage is good. Though rarer now, there are still public phones in Lisbon. With a phone card (available from post offices, newsagents, tobacconists and Portugal Telecom shops), they can be the cheapest option. There are fewer coin-operated phones, and they are less economical. All numbers within the country have nine digits. To call abroad, dial 00 and the country code first.

Internet Cafés and Wi-Fi Hotspots
Internet cafés in three main shopping centres – Columbo, Monumental and Vasco da Gama – are open from 10am to midnight seven days a week and charge around €2 per hour. Internet access is also available at PostNet and Unicâmbio centres dotted around the city. Most of these also offer Wi-Fi access. Other wireless hotspots are hotels, post offices, petrol stations and the airport. Ⓢ *NetCenter Cafe. Com: Rua do Diário de Notícias 157–9, Bairro Alto. Map K4 • K@netpoint: Columbo (opposite Benfica's Stadium of Light) • PostNet: Rua Braamcamp*

9, near Marquês Pombal. Map F3 • Unicâmbio: Praça da Figueira 2. Map M3

Newspapers and Magazines
Local dailies include *Público* and *Diário de Notícias*, both of which carry cinema listings.

Radio and TV
There is plenty of choice in music stations. Capital (100.8FM), RFM (93.2) and Antena 3 (100.3) are all middle of the road. Oxigénio (102.6), Mix (103) and Orbital (101.9) are more dance oriented. Marginal (98.1), Baía (98.7) and África (101.5) are mostly easy listening, while Antena 2 (94.4) is classical. The state-owned TV company is RTP: RTP 1 is commercial, with various sub-channels, and RTP 2 is culturally oriented. SIC, operating a plethora of channels, and TVI are private broadcasters. In Portugal foreign-language films are subtitled, not dubbed. Most hotels offer ample cable choice.

Speaking to the Locals
Portuguese can be challenging to the ear and those nasal endings hard to emulate, but no one will disapprove if you try. *Lisboetas* are proud of their language and mostly generous in interpreting it. Spanish is widely understood and so is English.

For listings publications **See p107**

Left **Raw fish brought to the table for inspection** Right **Tipping**

Top10 Eating, Lodging and Shopping

1 Reservations
It is always better to book a restaurant table in advance, though usually only necessary for dinner, weekend lunches and at the most popular places. A few restaurants do not take reservations, in which case arrive after 8pm to avoid a wait.

2 Meal Times
The Portuguese do not eat as late as the Spanish. Most restaurants open between 7pm and 8pm and close between 11pm and midnight. Lunch kicks off at around 1–2pm, and gets later and longer at weekends. During the week, a late lunch is a good way of avoiding a wait; for dinner, an early start has the same result.

3 Unrequested Appetizers
To varying degrees, all Portuguese restaurants place a selection of appetizers – usually cheeses, olives, bread and perhaps ham or salami – on the table before you order anything. These are often delicious, but they are not free. In many cheaper restaurants, they may end up doubling the cost of the meal. If you don't want to be tempted, just ask the waiter to remove them.

4 Choosing Dishes
Many restaurants have the laudable policy of displaying their meat and fish in glass-fronted refrigerators, allowing you to judge their quality and freshness. With fish, waiters will often bring the raw fish to the table for inspection. If you are in a hurry, or just hungry, order dishes listed as *pratos do dia*, dishes of the day. In general, fish is served with boiled potatoes and meat with chips and sometimes rice. However, this habit can be broken at the customer's request.

5 Portion Sizes
Traditional restaurants – and Lisbon still has many in this category – serve portions calculated to meet the calorie requirements of manual labourers rather than office workers or weight-conscious visitors. There is an established system of half portions – known as *meia dose* – that operates particularly at lunchtime. You get less food for your euros at more up-to-date restaurants, which serve smaller portions.

6 Tipping
A five to ten per cent tip is regarded as fairly generous after a meal in a restaurant. There is no obligation, and at lunch, in cafés or at bar counters, tips are much smaller.

7 Hotel Gradings
Hotels are graded with one to five stars, based on a fixed set of criteria covering most aspects of comfort. *Pensões* are classified from 3rd (lowest) to 1st (highest) grade, while the most luxurious are *albergaria*. Bear in mind that a one-, two- or even three-star hotel could be more basic than the top categories of *pensão*.

8 Hotel Prices
Most hotels' prices vary considerably over the year, and the margin for bargaining is quite large in Lisbon's now slightly over-supplied hotel market. It is also worth remembering that some of the business hotels regard summer as their low season.

9 Shop Hours
Shop hours are from 9am to 1pm and 2pm or 3pm to 7pm on weekdays. On Saturdays, shops are generally open until lunchtime and they close all day Sunday. The large shopping centres are an exception; many of their outlets are open throughout the day, until 10pm or 11pm, all week.

10 Bargaining
Bargaining is not common practice in shops, and attempts may be frowned upon – even when prices abundantly suggest it, as in antiques shops. Small "discounts" may sometimes be obtained for nebulous reasons, but the real bargaining is reserved for the casual market trade.

Left **Pretty but slippery cobbled pavement** Right **A rare port advertisement**

Things to Avoid

Rush Hour
The rush hour is roughly between 8:30am and 10am in the morning and 6pm and 8pm in the evening. While the trains are packed, the metro is much less affected. At peak times, it is best to allow about 40 minutes for the taxi ride to the airport from the centre.

Sintra at Weekends
Sintra *(see pp26–7)* suffers more than most from the weekend onslaught. Tour buses clog the roads and obscure the views, the queues to the main sights seem interminable, and cafés and restaurants are subject to frenzied rushes. In the week it is a different place – but bear in mind that the National Palace is closed on Wednesdays.

Driving in the City
Driving in Lisbon is generally unnecessary for visitors: distances are not huge, public transport covers most of the city and taxis are fairly cheap. Navigating its streets can be challenging – and Portuguese patience evaporates behind the wheel. Besides, the city is best discovered and enjoyed on foot. If you must drive, weekends are quieter than weekdays.

Thin-soled Shoes
Lisbon's pretty cobbled pavements are not even and get lethally slippery as soon as it starts to rain. If you intend to walk further than to the local restaurant, wear properly supportive, rubber-soled shoes.

Dog-fouled Pavements
The city's pavements can also be real minefields of dog mess, particularly in residential areas. Dog owners are only gradually starting to clean up after their pets. A few moped dog-mess hoovers are sporadically deployed.

Eating out on Sundays
A considerable proportion of Lisbon restaurants do not open on Sundays – and most of those that do close on Mondays instead. On either of these days, it is best to check with the restaurant before turning up.

Fado for Tourists
Fado represents a tourist obligation in Lisbon, which means that there is a market for packaging it in cost-effective ways. Culture loses on this, though, as does the experience you take away. Approach *fado* through the less grand *fado vadio* venues, then move on to the better fado restaurants *(see p43)* if you feel smitten by it.

Warmed Coffee
Lisbon is a city that takes its coffee seriously, but cafés indulge in one bad habit: keeping coffee warm for making the Portuguese equivalent of a *latte*, known as a *galão* and served in a tall glass. Ask for a *galão de máquina* to ensure that a freshly-made jet of coffee goes into yours.

Chip-fat Smell
Chips are a staple of Portuguese restaurants, and the deep-fat fryer is switched on throughout the day in most of them. In small, badly ventilated restaurants – that is, the majority – this may not be noticeable or particularly unpleasant at the time, but after leaving you will carry a strong smell of burnt deep-frying oil in your clothes. Some counter-measures include wearing a leather jacket; sitting outside; going to a sushi restaurant; or airing your clothes on your hotel balcony.

Port in the Wrong Places
It surprises many visitors that they don't see the Portuguese quaffing port in bars. Port is in fact mostly drunk at home, on special occasions. This means that most bars do not stock it, or if they do, that it is likely to be cheap, nasty and over-oxidized. Gourmet restaurants will always be serious about their port; alternatively you can head for the Port Wine Institute or Enoteca *(see p95)*.

A ban on smoking in public places, introduced in January 2008, has been relaxed to allow smoking in places with ventilation.

Left **Pestana Palace** Right **Tivoli Lisboa**

TOP 10 Luxury Hotels

1 Ritz Four Seasons
Few hotels can better this one for service. There may be luxury hotels in more attractive locations (though the roof-top running track is far removed from the traffic below) and with more characterful interiors (but take a look at the spa) – yet the Ritz is absolutely there for its guests. ⊗ *Rua Rodrigo da Fonseca 88 • Map F3 • 213 811 400 • www.four seasons.com/lisbon • €€€€€*

2 Olissippo Lapa Palace
Opulent and eclectic in its decor, this is now an established jewel in Lisbon's hotel crown. The location is quiet, but quite a walk from the centre. ⊗ *Rua do Pau da Bandeira 4 • Map E5 • 213 949 494 • www.olissippohotels.com • €€€€€*

3 Pestana Palace
Occupying a marvellously restored 19th-century palace with views of the Tagus, this grand hotel has extensions framing a garden. It is located between central Lisbon and Belém. ⊗ *Rua Jau 54 • Map G5 • 213 615 600 • www.pestana.com • €€€€€*

4 Avenida Palace
The doyen of the city's luxury hotels has a colourful history going back to the early 20th century. Since a major restoration, purists have

found it all a bit too mock-Belle Époque, but the location and atmosphere are hard to beat. ⊗ *Rua 1° de Dezembro 123 • Map L3 • 213 218 100 • www.hotel-avenida-palace.pt • €€€€*

5 Tivoli Lisboa
After half a century, Lisbon's original Tivoli hotel has earned the right to be called a classic. The vast lobby is an arcaded piazza that succeeds in being simultaneously grand and cosy. Another major attraction is the roof-top grill, with the views that most rooms lack. ⊗ *Avenida da Liberdade 185 • Map K1 • 213 198 900 • www. tivolihotels.com • €€€€€*

6 Sofitel Lisbon Liberdade
Ideally placed near Lisbon's commercial district and close to the main sights, the supremely stylish Sofitel is preferred by business executives for its modern conference facilities. ⊗ *Avenida da Liberdade 127 • Map K1 • 213 228 300 • www.sofitel.com • €€€€*

7 Real Palácio
Old and new blend easily here. A restored private palace, dating in its oldest parts back to the 17th century, adjoins a modern hotel building. The latter is filled with reproduction furnishings, but it is the palace, with its small patio, archways

and tiled stairwells, that is the highlight. ⊗ *Rua Tomás Ribeiro 115 • Map F2 • 213 199 500 • www.real hotelsgroup.com • €€€€€*

8 Tiara Park Atlantic Lisboa
In a modern building overlooking the Eduardo VII park, this is first and foremost a business hotel: comfortable, practical and professional. Some rooms on the higher floors have great views. ⊗ *Rua Castilho 149 • Map F2 • 213 818 700 • www. tiara-hotels.com • €€€€€*

9 Heritage Av Liberdade
Part of the small Heritage hotel group, this centrally located hotel is housed in a restored late 18th-century building. It is a showcase for Portuguese interior designer Miguel Câncio Martins, who mixes modernity with an oriental simplicity and warmth. ⊗ *Avenida da Liberdade 28 • Map F3 • 213 404 040 • www. heritage.pt • €€€€*

10 Hotel do Chiado
This medium-sized hotel has a privileged location. Some rooms have private verandas that look out over the Castelo de São Jorge *(see pp8–9)*, and down to the river. There is also a large veranda for all guests to enjoy. ⊗ *Rua Nova do Almada 114 • Map L4 • 213 256 100 • www. hoteldochiado.com • €€€*

Note: Unless otherwise stated, all hotels accept credit cards and have en-suite bathrooms and air conditioning

Duas Nações

Price Categories

For a standard,
double room per
night (with breakfast
if included), taxes
and extra charges.

€ under €50
€€ €50–€100
€€€ €100–€175
€€€€ €175–€250
€€€€€ over €250

🔟 Budget Hotels

1 Florescente
This place feels considerably more posh than the price suggests. It is also neater and cleaner than most of the competition. Dead-central location, parking facilities and free Wi-Fi Internet access enhance the good value that it offers. ✎ *Rua Portas de Santo Antão 99* • Map L2 • 213 426 609 • www.residencial florescente.com • €€

2 Londres
Longtime favourite of budget travellers, the Londres has gone upmarket. Cheaper rooms are still available – but the best one is at the top, overlooking Bairro Alto's warren of streets. ✎ *Rua Dom Pedro V 53, 2* • Map K2 • 213 462 203 • no air con • www.pensao londres.com.pt • €€

3 Alegria
The name Alegria, which translates as "joy", has often been said to refer to the girls of easy virtue who sometimes still venture to these parts. Conveniently located off the main drag but near the action, it offers fairly basic lodgings. ✎ *Praça da Alegria 12* • Map K2 • 213 220 670 • www.alegrianet.com • €

4 Horizonte
This comfortable, well-equipped, value-for-money *pensão* is in Lisbon's mid-town, near the Eduardo VII park and a short walk from the Gulbenkian *(see pp24–5)* and the Corte Inglés department store *(see p94)*. ✎ *Avenida António Augusto de Aguiar 42* • Map F2 • 213 539 526 • www. hotelhorizonte.com • €

5 Princesa
The setting for this cheap and comfortable *pensão* is a fairly central, but non-touristy part of the city. Downtown Lisbon is a lengthy downhill walk away; guests might want to return via the Elevador do Lavra *(see p66)* and the Psi café-restaurant *(see p95)*. Some rooms can be noisy. ✎ *Rua Gomes Freire 130* • Map G3 • 213 193 070 • www.residencial-princesa.pt • €

6 Globo
Located on a quiet Bairro Alto street, this basic and friendly *pensão* is an economical choice. The restaurant 100 Maneiras *(see p77)* is in the same street. ✎ *Rua do Teixeira 37* • Map K3 • 213 462 279 • no air con, no credit cards • www.pensaoglobo-lisbon.com • €

7 Alcantarense
Well placed for club-life in the Alcântara and Docas areas, this simple *pensão* caters mainly to business clients on a budget – some of the 17 rooms are always taken by long-term guests. For short stays, rooms can be had for as little as €35 a night. ✎ *Rua Vieira da Silva 119, 1D* • Map D5 • 213 966 552 • no air con, no credit cards • €

8 Ibérica
This is almost as cheap as it gets if you want your own room and a central location – right in the heart of things in this case. Your fellow guests are likely to be on a tight budget. A frugal place it may be, but not in any way threatening. ✎ *Praça da Figueira 10, 2* • Map M3 • 218 865 781 • no en-suite, no air con, no credit cards • €

9 Duas Nações
With a sometimes startling interior, but a good-natured atmosphere, this upmarket *pensão* occupies a grand old building in the Baixa. It is well-sited for compulsive shoppers, standing on a corner with the pedestrianized Rua Augusta. ✎ *Rua da Vitória 41* • Map M4 • 213 460 710 • no air con • www. duasnacoes.com • €€

10 Lar do Areeiro
Located north of the centre, this extremely comfortable *pensão* is near the Roma shopping district *(see p40)*, the Bela Vista park *(see p94)* and the airport. ✎ *Praça Francisco Sá Carneiro 4* • Map G1 • 218 493 150 • www.residenciallardo areeiro.com • €€

Prices are less negotiable in budget hotels; sometimes a haggle in a more expensive hotel will lead to the same price as a budget option.

Left **Bairro Alto** Right **York House**

🔟 Character Hotels

1 Palácio Belmonte
Eleven suites, each with its own character, occupy the city's oldest private palace, luxuriously restored with a near-manic attention to detail and historical authenticity. Buttressed on one side by Castelo de São Jorge (see pp8–9), the Belmonte offers fine views from its terraces and a small pool hidden from the public eye. The place is a dream, costing real money. ✆ Pátio Dom Fradique 14 • Map P4 • 218 816 600 • www.palacio belmonte.com • €€€€€

2 Bairro Alto
Set in an attractively restored 18th-century building in Praça de Camões, in the heart of Lisbon, this hotel delivers luxury with style. ✆ Praça Luís de Camões 2 • Map K4 • 213 408 288 • www. bairroaltohotel.com • €€€€€

3 Solar do Castelo
Once the kitchens of the original Alcáçovas Palace in Castelo de São Jorge (see pp8–9), then converted into a private palace in the 18th century, this is now a cosy, eclectically furnished boutique hotel around a small courtyard. ✆ Rua das Cozinhas 2 • Map N3 • 218 806 050 • www.heritage.pt • €€€€

4 Quinta Nova da Conceição
This 18th-century summer residence – it was then far beyond the limits of the city – is still owned by the same family and has an atmosphere few character hotels can match. Book early, as there are only three rooms. ✆ Rua Cidade de Rabat 5 • Map B2 • 217 780 091 • www.quintanova conceicao.com • €€€

5 York House
A former 17th-century convent, turned into a boarding house by two Yorkshire women in the 19th century. Graham Greene stayed here, when rates were lower and the furnishings less stylish. The place hasn't lost its character – the dark corridors could come from a story by Borges. ✆ Rua das Janelas Verdes 32 • Map E5 • 213 962 435 • www.yorkhouselisboa. com • €€€€

6 Olissippo Castelo
Beautifully located beneath Castelo de São Jorge, with views across the city, this is the pride of the small Olissippo hotels group. It provides extreme comfort in light, airy, textile-rich rooms. ✆ Rua Costa do Castelo 126 • Map N3 • 218 820 190 • www.olissippohotels. com • €€€€

7 Metropole
Decorated with real Art-Nouveau pieces as well as reproductions, the Metropole has a genuine feel and a superb central location overlooking Rossio. As part of the Almeida chain, it has the bonus of offering prized wines from the Bussaco Palace Hotel. ✆ Praça Dom Pedro IV (Rossio) 30 • Map L3 • 213 219 030 • www. almeidahotels.com • €€€

8 Britânia
Well placed in a quiet street just off Avenida da Liberdade, the Britânia is a gem with a style all its own. Housed in a 1940s building, it combines wood and marble in its Art Deco design and goes easy on the textiles. ✆ Rua Rodrigues Sampaio 17 • Map F3 • 213 155 016 • www.heritage.pt • €€€€

9 Casa de São Mamede
This atmospheric if somewhat hushed pensão has a good location slightly off the main tourist track. Set in a grand 18th-century residence, it gives a taste of an older Lisbon. ✆ Rua da Escola Politécnica 159 • Map F3 • 213 963 166 • No Am Ex • www. saomamede.web.pt • €€

10 Inspira Santa Marta
Designed as an urban retreat, the four-star Inspira Santa Marta combines a noble 19th-century façade with an eye-catching minimalist interior. It has won awards for its ecologically sustainable practices. ✆ Rua de Santa Marta 48 • Map F3 • 210 440 900 • www.inspira santamartahotel.com • €€€

Note: Unless otherwise stated, all hotels accept credit cards and have en-suite bathrooms and air conditioning

Price Categories

For a standard, double room per night (with breakfast if included), taxes and extra charges.

€	under €50
€€	€50–€100
€€€	€100–€175
€€€€	€175–€250
€€€€€	over €250

Solar dos Mouros

TOP 10 Rooms with a View

1 Albergaria Senhora do Monte

Set on one of Lisbon's highest hills, this relatively plain hotel boasts some of the city's best views. It's a quiet perch for the walking, atmosphere-absorbing visitor. ⓢ Calçada do Monte 39 • Map P1 • 218 866 002 • www.albergariasenhorado monte.com • €€€

2 Sheraton

A landmark on the city's modest skyline, the Sheraton has beautiful views from its rather 1970s interior. A business hotel, it offers five-star comfort at reasonable rates and a panoramic roof-top restaurant. ⓢ Rua Latino Coelho 1 • Map F2 • 213 120 000 • www.sheraton.com • €€€€

3 Dom Pedro

This lofty glass pile in the Amoreiras business and shopping district features traditional, textile-heavy luxury – with the exception of some of the suites. Views from almost every room are stunning. ⓢ Avenida Engenheiro Duarte Pacheco 24 • Map E3 • 213 896 600 • www.dompedro.com • €€€€€

4 Mundial

Superbly located in downtown Lisbon, the eight-floor Mundial has views across the Baixa and up towards the castle. Comfortable rooms serve their purpose and have large windows that open:

a potential hazard for children. The roof-top restaurant is popular with local politicians. ⓢ Praça Martim Moniz 2 • Map M3 • 218 842 000 • www.hotel-mundial.pt • €€€

5 Eduardo VII

Just off the park of the same name (and the busy Marquês de Pombal roundabout), the Best Western Eduardo VII offers good value and great views from many of its pleasant, if small, rooms. A panoramic restaurant and a clubby bar complete the picture. ⓢ Avenida Fontes Pereira de Melo 5 • Map F2 • 213 568 800 • www.hotel eduardovii.pt • €€€

6 Tryp Oriente

This purpose-built hotel by Parque das Nações (see pp16–17) provides modern facilities, plus views of the wide Tejo estuary from light, airy rooms. The location gives easy access to the airport. It is part of the Sol Meliá chain. ⓢ Avenida Dom João II • Map C1 • 218 930 000 • www.tryporiente.com • €€€

7 Altis Belém Hotel & Spa

Lisbon's first five-star riverfront hotel commands uninterrupted views of the Tejo. It's also noted for its cutting-edge interior design. ⓢ Doca do Bom Sucesso • Map A6 • 210 400 200 • www.altisbelemhotel.com • €€€

8 Chiado 16

This charming boutique hotel houses a series of exclusive and beautifully appointed apartments that feature fully equipped kitchens and marble bathrooms. The interior is embellished with vintage film posters, but the views are the real scene-stealers. ⓢ Largo da Academia das Belas Artes 16 • Map L5 • 213 941 616 • www.chiado16.com • €€€€€

9 Ninho das Águias

This has to be one of the city's most attractive pensões, for the wonderful old building itself, its large terrace, its turret, its location just below the castle walls and the views (which are, however, away from the river). Rooms are basic, though, and a long climb up a spiral staircase. ⓢ Rua Costa do Castelo 74 • Map N3 • 218 854 070 • no en-suite, no air con, no credit cards • €

10 Solar dos Mouros

Located on the remains of one of the Moorish-era gates to Castelo de São Jorge, this small hotel has simply but tastefully decorated rooms. Contemporary art from the owner's private collection features prominently, as do views of the city and the river. ⓢ Rua do Milagre de Santo António 6 • Map N4 • 218 854 940 • www.solardos mouros.com • €€€€

For some of Lisbon's many viewing points See pp36–7

Streetsmart

Left **Seteais Palace, near Sintra** Right **Fortaleza do Guincho**

🔟 Lisbon Coast Hotels

1 Albatroz
Central Cascais' most characterful hotel has a to-die-for location on a promontory with sandy beaches to either side. The main building typifies the summer villas built here for aristocrats in the 19th century. The Italianate Albatroz Palace across the street is also part of the hotel. ✪ *Rua Frederico Arouca 100, Cascais • 214 847 380 • www.albatroz hotels.com • €€€€€*

2 Casa da Pérgola
With its two-tone mansard roof, curving eaves and tiled window surrounds, this elegant bed and breakfast in central Cascais is unmistakable. The garden is also dazzling. ✪ *Avenida Valbom 13, Cascais • 214 840 040 • www.palacio house.com • €€€*

3 Palácio Estoril
Still with a whiff of Estoril's heyday as a glamorous resort, the Palácio was built in the 1930s and former guests range from royalty to spies. Its enduring grandeur is attested by its interiors and service. ✪ *Rua Particular, Estoril • 214 648 000 • www.palacio estorilhotel.com • €€€€€*

4 Farol Design
Within an extended villa overlooking the sea, this modern luxury hotel has interiors designed by top names in Portuguese fashion. For all the design hype, the main attraction is that some rooms have floor-to-ceiling windows, giving you the feeling of crawling into bed at sea. ✪ *Avenida Rei Humberto II de Itália 7, Cascais • 214 823 490 • www.farol.com.pt • €€€€€*

5 Senhora da Guia
Just outside central Cascais and a chip away from the Quinta da Marinha golf course, this hotel embodies civilized luxury with a slightly English touch. It has a salt-water pool. ✪ *Estrada do Guincho, Cascais • 214 869 239 • www.senhora daguia.com • €€€€€*

6 Palácio Seteais
One of the many gems of the Sintra region, this palatial hotel was built for a Dutch diplomat in 1787; its Neo-Classical façade and triumphal arch were added later. Now part of the Tivoli chain, it offers the usual luxuries and an inimitable atmosphere. ✪ *Rua Barbosa du Bocage 8–10, Sintra • 219 233 200 • www.tivoli hotels.com • €€€€€*

7 Lawrence's
Dating from 1764, this charming hotel on the edge of Sintra town claims to be the oldest on the Iberian peninsula. Some of its individually furnished rooms are named after famous guests, among them Lord Byron. The restaurant is run with a real passion.
✪ *Rua Consiglieri Pedroso 38–40, Sintra • 219 105 500 • www.lawrenceshotel.com • €€€€*

8 Quinta da Capela
Low, simple, ochre-glowing buildings; gardens of neatly clipped hedges framing gravel paths – you could almost be in Umbria. The interior is elegant and restrained. ✪ *Estrada Velha de Colares • 219 290 170 • www. quintadacapela.com • €€€€*

9 Fortaleza do Guincho
Housed in an old fortress, on a cliff by Guincho beach, this hotel makes good use of the romantic potential of its windswept location, vaulted rooms and grand staircases. Best of all are the junior suites, with arcaded terraces facing the Atlantic. The restaurant has one Michelin star. ✪ *Estrada do Guincho, Cascais • 214 870 491 • www.guinchotel. pt • €€€€€*

10 Saboia
Among Estoril's mid-price hotels, this one has the advantage that all its rooms have balconies – most, but not all, have sea views. Rooms are plain but comfortable. The location is handy for access to both Cascais and Estoril, and the train station is short but steep walk away. ✪ *Rua do Belmonte 1, Monte Estoril • 214 680 202 • www. saboiaestorilhotel.com • €€*

Note: Unless otherwise stated, all hotels accept credit cards and have en-suite bathrooms and air conditioning

Price Categories

For a standard, double room per night (with breakfast if included), taxes and extra charges.

€ under €50
€€ €50–€100
€€€ €100–€175
€€€€ €175–€250
€€€€€ over €250

Streetsmart

Avenida Parque

🔟 Self-catering, Family and Camping

1 VIP Executive Suites Eden

Housed in what was the grand Art Deco Eden theatre, overlooking Restauradores, this is Lisbon's most central and well-equipped aparthotel. The rooftop pool has great views over the city. Ⓢ Praça dos Restauradores 24 • Map L2 • 213 216 600 • www.viphotels.com • €€€

2 Tivoli Jardim

Centrally located, just behind the main Tivoli (see p112), reasonably priced and with a round swimming pool, this is a good option for families – albeit one that is also popular with business people. Ⓢ Rua Júlio César Machado 7–9 • Map F3 • 213 591 000 • www.tivolihotels.com • €€€

3 Avenida Parque

Just off Parque Eduardo VII (see p91), this hotel offers good value and a practical location. Most rooms overlook the park; some have balconies. Ⓢ Avenida Sidónio Pais 6 • Map F2 • 213 532 181 • www.avenidaparquehotel.com • €€

4 Roma

A pensão residencial, the Roma has 25 rooms and 12 small apartments equipped with kitchen- ettes. It's a basic place, but sound and clean, and the location is great, just around the corner from the Elevador da Glória

(see p73). The apartments are on the third and fourth floors of the building; there is no lift. Ⓢ Travessa da Glória 22A • Map K2 • 213 460 557 • www.residenciaroma.com • €€

5 Clarion Suites

This well-equipped mid-range hotel is to be found near the Marquês de Pombal roundabout. Standard suites are small and have kitchenettes. More swish penthouse suites are also available. Ⓢ Rua Rodrigo da Fonseca 44 • Map F3 • 210 046 600 • www.choice hotelseurope.com • €€€

6 Real Residência

Comprising 22 suites and two studios, all with kitchenettes, this suite hotel stands just across the street from the Gulbenkian Museum (see pp24–5), while Parque Eduardo VII is a few blocks away. Guests have access to the health club at sister hotel the Real Palácio (see p112), which is located a bit farther away. Ⓢ Rua Ramalho Ortigão 41 • Map F1 • 213 822 900 • www.realhotelsgroup.com • €€€

7 Altis Suites

Offering holiday apartments in a central location, this aparthotel is part of the Portuguese Altis chain. It comes with all amenities such as 24-hour reception desk, restaurant, indoor pool and health club and has a

family-oriented staff. Ⓢ Rua Castilho 13 • Map F3 • 213 191 400 • www.altishotels.com • €€€

8 Lisboa Camping

Lisbon's main campsite is located in the Monsanto park (see p83), immediately west of the centre. Well equipped in practical as well as leisure terms, it can get crowded in the summer, particularly at weekends. Those who prefer a solid roof over their heads can rent a bungalow. Ⓢ Estrada Circunvalação • Map B3 • 217 628 200 • www.lisboacamping.com • €

9 Camping Orbitur, Guincho

Attractively located among umbrella pines behind the dunes of Guincho beach, this campsite is popular with surfers. Among its facilities is a tennis court. Bungalows are available. Ⓢ Estrada da Areia, Cascais • 214 870 450 • www.orbitur.pt • €

10 Camping Orbitur, Costa da Caparica

Situated near the northern end of the Caparica coast, this campsite set among pines is just 200 m (220 yards) from the beach. Many lisboetas have semi-permanent set ups here, and it can get pretty crowded in the summer. Ⓢ Avda Afonso de Albuquerque, Quinta S António • 212 901 366 • www.orbitur.pt • €

General Index

Page numbers in **bold** type refer to main entries.

31 da Armada 51

A
A Brasileira 75
A Carioca 74
Aché Cohiba 76
activities, outdoor 49
Adaptacar 108
Adega das Mercês 77
Adega do Kais 89
Adraga 49
Afonso Henriques, King 31
    Castelo de São Jorge 8, 9
    Reconquest 30
    Sintra 26
    statue of 8
African Lisbon 38–9
Agência 117 74
A Ginjinha 68
Água no Bico 87
airport 106
Alameda 94
Alan tribes 30
Albatroz 116
Albergaria Senhora do
    Monte 115
Alcácer do Sal 52
Alcáçovas palace 8
Alcântara Café 89
Alcântara-Mar 42, 88
Alcantarense 113
Alecrim às Flores 77
Alegria 113
Alfama, Castelo and the
    East 56–61
    bars and cafes 60
    map 56
    restaurants 61
    walk in 59
Alfândega – Armazém dos
    Sabores 69
A Licorista 68
Altis Belém Hotel & Spa
    115
Altis Suites 117
Alto de Santa Catarina 36
Alves, Manuel 74
Amaral, Keil do 93
Amazéns do Chiado 74
ambulances 108
American Embassy 107
Amoreiras 40
Ana Salazar 74

Angola 39
Anthony of Padua, St 13,
    33, 58
Anthony, St (Egyptian
    saint) 82
Antiga Confeitaria de
    Belém 45, 86
Antiga Ervanária
    d'Anunciada 66
appetizers, unrequested
    110
aquarium 16, 50
Aqueduto das Águas
    Livres 82–3
Arco do Castelo 61
Aromi 103
Arruda, Francisco de 18
Arte Rústica 66
Artis 76
artists 35
A Severa 43
Assembleia da República
    81
Associação Caboverdeana
    38
Associação Católica
    Internacional ao Serviço
    da Juventude Feminina
    77
Assuka 95
A Travessa 44, 89
Australian Embassy 107
Autódromo do Estoril
    102
Avenida & North Lisbon
    90–95
    map 90
    restaurants and cafés 95
    walks 93
Avenida da Liberdade 41
Avenida designer shops 94
Avenida Palace 112
Avenida Parque 117
Avenidas Novas 91
Aya Bistrôt 89
Azeitão 52
Azenhas do Mar 102
Azevedo Rua 67
Aziz 38
Azulejo, Museu Nacional
    do 7, **20–21**, 34, 59

B
Bairro Alto 40, 114
    see also Chiado &
    Bairro Alto

Baixa to Restauradores
    62–9
    bars and cafes 68
    map 62
    restaurants 69
    shops 40, 67
    walks 65
Bana 38
banking 109
Bar 106, 87
Bar das Avencas 103
Bar das Imagens 8, 60
Bar Lounge 42, 88
Bar do Rio 43
bargaining 110
bars 42–3
    Alfama, Castelo and the
    East 60
    Baixa to Restauradores
    68
    Gay Lisbon 87
Basílica da Estrela 32,
    83
beaches 48–9, 51
    safety 108
beauty spots 53
beauty treatments 41
Bedroom 76
Belém 83
    see also West Lisbon
Belém, Torre de 7, **18–19**,
    33, 84
Belém Bar Café 42, 85
Bénard 45, 75
Benfica 94
Berardo, José 34
Berardo Collection 34, 84
Berbers 31
Bica do Sapato 44, 61
bicycles 49
bird-watching 49
board sports 49
boats
    ferries 106
    sailing 49
Boca do Inferno 102
Boitac, Diogo 10, 12, 18
Bonjardim Rei dos Frangos
    69
Bosch, Hieronymus, The
    Temptations of St
    Anthony 14, 82
Bragança, Duke of see
    João IV, Dom
Bragança family 32
Brazil 39

Bric-a-Bar 87
Britânia 114
British Bar 68
British Embassy 107
Bucelas 53
budget hotels 113
Bulhão, Fernando Martins 13
bullfighting 92
buses 106
Byron, Lord 7, 27, 116

C
cable cars 17
Cabo Espichel 53
Cabo da Roca 100, 101
Caetano, Marcelo 31, 71
Café Buenos Aires 51, 77
Café Luso 43
Café Martinho da Arcada 68
Café Mexicana 45, 95
cafés 45
    Alfama, Castelo and the East 60
    Avenida & North Lisbon 95
    Baixa to Restauradores 68
Cafetaria de São Carlos 75
Cais de Belém 85
Calçada do Duque 72–3
Camões, Luís de
    Cabo da Roca 100
    The Lusiads 36
    Praça Luís de Camões 72
    tomb of 10, 11
camping 117
Camping Orbitur (Costa da Caparica) 117
Camping Orbitur (Guincho) 117
Campo de Ourique 40, 83
Campo Pequeno 91
Campo de Santa Clara 59
Canadian Embassy 107
Cantinho da Paz 39
Cantinho do Aziz 38
Caparica Centre 48
Caparica North 48
Cape Verde Association 38
Cape Verde islands 39
Capela 76
Capela de Bartolomeu Joanes 13
Carcavelos 48
Carlos, Dom 30
Carmo 32, 73

Carnation Revolution (1974) 31
cars
    driving in Lisbon 111
    driving to Lisbon 106
    safety 108
Cartão do Parque 17
Casa do Alentejo 44, 69
Casa dos Bicos 33
Casa do Fado e da Guitarra Portuguesa 58
Casa Fernando Pessoa 81, 83
Casa do Leão 9, 61
Casa de Linhares 43
Casa da Morna 38
Casa da Pérgola 116
Casa de São Mamede 114
Casanostra 77
Casanova 51, 61
Cascais 48, 101
Cascais Cultural Centre 102
Cascais-Estoril Waterfront 99
Cascais Marina 99
cash dispensers 109
Casino 16
Castelo 36
    see also Alfama, Castelo and the East
Castelo dos Mouros (Sintra) 26, 53
Castelo de São Jorge 6, **8–9**, 57
Castilho, João de 10, 33
Castro, Joaquim Machado de 13, 35, 63
Catacumbas 76
Cathedral 6, **12–13**, 32, 57
Catherine the Great, Empress of Russia 25
CCB see Centro Cultural de Belém
Ceilão 39
Cenáculo 31
Centro Cultural de Belém (CCB) 86
ceramics
    Museu Nacional do Azulejo 7, **20–21**, 34, 59
    things to buy 41
Cerca Moura 60
Cervejaria Solmar 69
Cervejaria Trindade 73
Chanterène, Nicolau 10\
Chá Do Carmo 75

Chapel of St Albert 15
Chapitô 60
character hotels 114
Chiado 16, 115
Chiado & Bairro Alto 70–77
    bars 76
    cafés 75
    map 70
    restaurants 77
    shops 40, 74
    walks 73
children 50–51, 107
Christian Reconquest 30
churches and monasteries 32–3
cinema 51
city views 36–7
Clarion Suites 117
climate 107
clothes, things to buy 41
Clube da Esquina 76
Clube de Fado 43
Clube de Jornalistas 89
CNAD 108
Coach Museum 34, 84
coast see Lisbon coast
Coconuts 102
coffee 111
Coisas do Arco do Vinho 86
Colares 101
Colares wine 100
Colombo shopping centre 50, 94
colonies 39
Columbus, Christopher 30
communications 109
Conceição Velha Portal 33
Confeitaria Nacional 45, 68
Conserveira de Lisboa 65, 66
Convento dos Capuchos 100, 101
Convento do Carmo 71
cookware, stainless steel 41
El Corte Inglés 94
Costa da Caparica, camping 117
credit cards 109
crime 108
Cristo Rei 37
Cruzes da Sé 59
culinary highlights 46–7
Culturgest 35, 94
currency 109
currency exchange 109

customs limits 107
Cutileiro, João 35, 93
cycling 49

D

Das Maçãs 49
D'Avis 61
Deli Delux 60
Design Museum 27, 34, 84, 86
Dinis, Dom 53
disabled travellers 108
Discoteca Amália 55
discounts, Cartão do Parque 17
Doca de Santo Amaro, restaurants 51
Docas area 86
doctors 108
dog-fouled pavements 111
Dom Grelhas 103
Dom Pedro 115
drinks *see* food and drinks; wines
Duas Nações 113
Dürer, Albrecht, *St Jerome* 14

E

earthquake (1755) 30, 62, 63
Eduardo VII Hotel 115
Eduardo VII park 37
Edward VII, King of England 91
Eiffel, Gustave 64
Elevador da Bica 72, 73
Elevador da Glória 73
Elevador do Lavra 66
Elevador de Santa Justa 37, 64
Eleven 44, 93, 95
embassies 107
embroidery, things to buy 41
Enclave 38–9
English-language newspapers 107
Enoteca 95
Enoteca de Belém 85
Ermida de Santo Amaro 82
Ermida de São Jerónimo 33
Espaço Lisboa 44
Esplanada da Igreja da Graça 60
Esporão wine 47
Estádio José Alvalade 92

Estado Líquido 88
Estádio da Luz 92
Estoril 48
Estoril Casino 99
Estoril Mandarim 103
Estoril Waterfront 99
Estrela 81
Estufa Real 85
Etílico 76
European Union 31
Euros 109
ex-colonies 39
excursions 52–3

F

Fábrica da Pólvora 102
fado 111
    Museu do Fado 58
    venues 43
family accommodation 117
Farol Design 116
Faz Figura 61
Feira da Ladra 41, 59
Fernando II, Dom 26, 27
Ferreira wine 47
ferries 106
Festas da Cidade 58
Festas dos Santos Populares 58
Fielding, Henry 81
Finalmente 87
fish, poisonous 108
fishing 49
Florescente 113
food and drinks
    coffee 111
    culinary highlights 46–7
    fresh food markets 40
    things to buy 41
    see also restaurants; wines
football stadiums 92
Fortaleza do Guincho 103, 116
Four Seasons Grill 103
Foxtrot 88
Frágil 87
Fronteira, 12th Marquis of 93
Fundação/Museu Arpad Szenes-Vieira da Silva 35, 86
Fundação Ricardo do Espírito Santo Silva 59
funicular railways 106
    Elevador da Bica 72, 73
    Elevador da Glória 73
    Elevador do Lavra 66

funicular railways (cont.)
    Elevador de Santa Justa 37, 64
Fusion 95

G

Galeria 111 34
galleries *see* museums and galleries
Gama, Vasco da
    Parque das Nações 16
    tomb of 11
    voyage to India 30
Gambrinus 69
gardens *see* parks and gardens
gay Lisbon 87
George, St 8
Gilbert of Hastings 57
Globo 113
Goa 39
golf courses, Lisbon coast 102
Gonçalves, José Manuel 74
Gonçalves, Nuno 35
    The Adoration of St Vincent 14, 34, 35
Graça 33
Grande 49
Guerra Junqueiro, Avda 40
Guincho 99
    beach 48–9
    camping 117
    scenic coast road 53
Guinea-Bissau 39
Gulbenkian, Calouste 24, 25, 34, 91

H

haberdashers in Rua da Conceição 66
health 108
Henriques, Dom Afonso 12
Henry the Navigator 31
    Padrão dos Descombrimentos 84
    statues of 10
    tomb of 10, 11
Herculano, Alexandre 11
Heritage Av Liberdade 112
history 30–31
holidays, public 107
Hooch, Pieter de, *Conversation* 14
Horizonte 113
horse riding 49

Hospital de Bonecas 67
hospitals 108
Hot Clube 94
Hotel do Chiado 112
hotels 112–17
    booking 107
    budget hotels 113
    character hotels 114
    gradings 110
    Lisbon coast 116
    luxury hotels 112
    prices 110
    rooms with a view 115
Houdon, Jean-Antoine,
    Diana Statue 25

I
Ibérica 113
ice skating 50–51
Igreja da Conceição Velha
    63, 65
Igreja da Graça 36
Igreja da Memória 86
Igreja de Santa Engrácia
    58–9
Igreja de São Domingos
    64, 65
Igreja de São Miguel 59
Igreja de São Roque 72,
    73
In Rio Lounge 85
Incógnito 42, 88
Indian Embassy 107
Indochina 88
Inspira Santa Marta 114
insurance, health 108
Internet 107
Internet cafés 109
Irish Embassy 107
Isabel of Aragon 53

J
Jamaica 43
Jardim Botânico 81
Jardim Botânico da Ajuda
    86
Jardim da Estrela 83
Jardim dos Sentidos 51
Jardim do Torel 37
Jardim do Torel (café) 95
Jardim Museu Agrícola
    Tropical 84
Jardim Zoológico 50, 93
Jerónimos, Mosteiro dos
    6, **10–11**, 32, 33, 84
Jesuits 33, 72
Joalharia Correia 67
João I, Dom 64

João IV, Dom 30, 31
João V, Dom 52, 72, 84
João Portugal Ramos wine
    47
jogging 49
José I, Dom 31
    Igreja da Memória 86
    statue of 35, 63

K
Kaffeehaus 75
Kais 89
Knowledge Pavilion –
    Ciência Viva 16, 50, 93
Koëlla, Léon-Édouard 25
Kremlin 42, 88

L
Labyrinto 87
Lagoa de Albufeira 48
Lalique, René 25
language 109
Lapa streets 86
Lar do Areeiro 113
Largo 77
Largo do Chafariz do
    Dentro 59
Largo and Convento do
    Carmo 71
Largo das Portas do Sol 57
Largo de São Domingos
    66
Largo de São Miguel 57
Laurentina 45
Lautasco 61
Lawrence's Hotel (Sintra)
    26, 116
Leão d'Ouro 69
Leitão & Irmão 74
Leitaria Académica 75
Leitaria Caneças 45
Leo X, Pope 63
Leonor, Dona 63
Linha d'Água 93
Lisboa Camping 117
Lisboa Welcome Centre
    107
Lisbon coast 98–103
    hotels 116
    map 98
    restaurants 103
    Sintra drive 101
    trains 106
Lisbonense 67
listings publications 107
Livraria Bertrand 74
Londres 113
Lusitanians 31

Luvaria Ulisses 74
Lux 42
luxury hotels 112

M
Das Maçãs 49
Macau 39
Madre de Deus Church 20
Mafra 52–3
magazines 109
    listings publications 107
Magnolia Caffé 95
Malhoa, José 35
Manet, Édouard, Boy
    Blowing Bubbles 25
Manifesto 45
Manuel I, Dom 11, 63, 84
Manuel II, Dom 30
Manuel Tavares 67
Manueline architecture 33
Maria I, Dona
    Basílica da Estrela 32
    Palácio de Queluz 22, 23
    tomb of 11, 32
Maria II, Dona 26
markets, food 40
Martinho da Arcada 69
Matos, Marçal de 21
Maxime 94
Maximilian, Emperor of
    Mexico 64
meal times 110
Meco 48
medical treatment 108
Memorial 87
Mercado 31 de Janeiro 40
Mercado da Campo de
    Ourique 40
Mercado da Ribeira 40
Mercado de Santa Clara
    61
Metro 106
Metropole 114
Miradouro de Santa
    Catarina 86
Moamba 39
mobile phones 109
monasteries and churches
    32–3
La Moneda 45
money 109
Monitz, Martim 9
Monsanto 50, 83
Monserrate 27, 53, 100–101
Monte Estoril 99
Monteiro, António
    Augusto Carvalho 27,
    102

Moors 30
Mosteiro dos Jerónimos 6, **10–11**, 32, 33, 84
mountain biking 49
Mozambique 39
Mundial 115
Museu de Arqueologia 11, 84
Museu do Brinquedo 27
Museu Calouste Gulbenkian 7, **24–5**, 34, 91, 93
Museu do Chiado 35, 71
Museu da Cidade 92
Museu de Ciência 51
Museu Collecção Berardo Arte Moderna e Contemporânea 34, 84
Museu Condes de Castro Guimarães 102
Museu do Design e da Moda (MUDE) 66
Museu do Fado 58
Museu da Marinha 11, 84
Museu da Marioneta 82
Museu Nacional de Arte Antiga 6, **14–15**, 34, 82, 83
Museu Nacional do Azulejo 7, **20–21**, 33, 34, 59
Museu Nacional dos Coches 34, 84
Museu Rafael Bordalo Pinheiro 94
Museu de São Roque 72
Museu do Teatro Romano 57
museums and galleries 34–5
music
    fado 43, 111
    Museu do Fado 58
Mussulo 39

N
Napoleão 67
Napoleon I, Emperor 22, 23
Nariz de Vinho Tinto 14, 89
Nautical Centre 17
Nectar Wine Bar 68
newspapers 109
    English-language 107
Nicola 68
Niepoort wine 47
nightclubs 42–3

nightclubs (cont.)
    West Lisbon (with Belém) 88
Ninho das Águias 115
No Chiado 75
North Lisbon see Avenida & North Lisbon
Nosolo Itália 51, 85
Nossa Senhora da Vida altarpiece 21
Núcleo Arqueológico da Rua dos Correeiros 63
La Nuit des Musées 15

O
O Bacalhoeiro 69
O Chá da Lapa 45
O Faia 43
O Mercado 89
O Moinho 101
O Pereira 103
Óbidos 53
Óbidos, Josefa de 35
Oceanarium 16, 50
O'Gilin's 68, 73
Olissippo Castelo 114
Olissippo Lapa Palace 112
Ondajazz Bar 60
100 Maneiras 77
Op Art 43
opening hours 110
Oriente 77
Os Ferreiras 43
Os Jerónimos 85
outdoor activities 49

P
Pacheco, Lopo Fernandes 12
Pacheco, Mário 43
Padrão dos Descobrimentos 84
Paiva, Gaspar de 18
Palácio da Ajuda 84
Palácio de Belém 84
Palácio Belmonte 114
Palácio Estoril 116
Palácio dos Marqueses da Fronteira 93
Palácio Nacional de Sintra 26
Palácio Nacional da Pena (Sintra) 26
Palácio de Queluz 7, **22–3**
Palácio de Seteais 27
Palácio Seteais Hotel 116
Palmela 52

Pancas 53
Panificação Mecânica 45
Panteão Nacional 58–9
Pap'Açorda 77
Papagaio da Serafina 51
La Paparrucha 73
Paradise Garage 42, 88
Paris, Tito 38
"Park of the Nations" 16–17
parks and gardens
    Castelo de São Jorge 9
    Jardim Botânico 81
    Jardim Botânico da Ajuda 86
    Jardim da Estrela 81, 83
    Jardim do Torel 37
    Jardim do Ultramar 84
    Monsanto 50, 83
    Monserrate 27, 100–101
    Parque Eduardo VII 37, 91, 93
    Parque do Monteiro-Mor 92
    Parque das Nações 7, **16–17**, 51, 93
    Parque da Pena 102
Paródia 88
Parque da Bela Vista 94
Parque da Liberdade 27
Parque da Pena (Sintra) 27
Parreirinha de Alfama 43
passports 107
Pastelaria Versailles 45, 95
pastelarias (pastry shops) 45
Pau de Canela 45
pavements, dog-fouled 111
Pavilhão Chinês 76
Pedro, Prince 22
Pedro IV, Dom 64
Penedo 53
Peninha 53, 101, 102
Pessoa, Fernando 65, 81
Pestana Palace 112
pharmacies 108
Philip II, King of Spain 32
phone cards 109
Picanha de Belém 85
pickpockets 108
PIDE 31
Piero della Francesca, St Augustine 14
Pinheiro, Columbano Bordalo 35
Pinheiro, Rafael Bordalo 94

Poço dos Negros area 38
Pois, Café 12, 60
poisonous fish 108
police 108
Pollux 67
Pomar, Júlio 34, 35
Pombal 70
Pombal, Marquês de 31, 63
   statue of 90, 91, 93
Ponsard, Raoul Mesnier de 64
Ponte 25 de Abril 82
Ponte Salazar 82
port 111
Port Wine Institute 73
Porta de São Jorge 8
Portas Largas 76
Portela airport 106
Portinho da Arrábida 53
Porto de Santa Maria 103
Portugal Pavilion 16
Portuguese language 109
post offices 109
Praça do Comércio 63, 65
Praça da Figueira 64, 65
Praça dos Restauradores 65
Praça Luís de Camões 72
Prazeres 83
Princesa 113
Psi 51, 95
public holidays 107
Puppet Museum 82

Q
Queiroz, Eça de 31
Queluz, Palácio de 7, **22–3**
Quinta da Capela 116
Quinta do Crasto wine 47
Quinta do Monte d'Oiro wine 47
Quinta Nova da Conceição 114
Quinta Pedagógica 50
Quinta da Pellada wine 47
Quinta da Regaleira 27, 101
Quinta do Vale Meão wine 47

R
radio 109
railway stations 106
Real Fábrica 44
Real Palácio 112

Real Residència 117
Reconquest 30
Rego, Paula 34, 35
Reis, Soares dos 8
Rembrandt, *Portrait of an Old Man* 25
Republic 30
Restauradores *see* Baixa to Restauradores
restaurants 44–5
   Alfama, Castelo and the East 61
   appetizers 110
   Avenida & North Lisbon 95
   Baixa to Restauradores 69
   Chiado & Bairro Alto 77
   choosing dishes 110
   eating out on Sundays 111
   family-friendly 51
   Lisbon coast 103
   opening hours 110
   portion sizes 110
   reservations 110
   tipping 110
   West Lisbon 85, 89
   see also food and drink
Ribadouro 95
Ribatejo Wine Route 53
Ritz Four Seasons 112
road travel 106
Roberto, Frei 12
Robillon, Jean-Baptiste 22
roller skating 49, 50–51
Roma, Avda 40
Roma, Pensão 117
Romans 30
Rossio 64
Rossio Station 33, 66
Rotunda Marquês de Pombal 91
Royale 75
Rua do Arsenal 66
Rua Augusta 63
Rua do Carmo 71
Rua da Conceição 66
Rua Dom Antão de Almada 65
Rua dos Douradoures 65
Rua de Escola Politécnica 41
Rua Garrett 71
Rua das Portas de Santo Antão 65
Rua de Rosa 73

Rua de São Bento 41
Rua de São João da Praça 59
Rua de São Pedro 59
Rua Vieira Portuense, restaurants 51
rush hour 111

S
Saboia 116
Sacramento 75
safety 108
sailing 49
Salazar, António de Oliveira 31, 82
Salto Alto 76
Santa Apolónia 41, 59
Santa Cruz neighbourhood 9
Santa Engrácia 32
Santa Luzia 36
Santiago Alquimista 60
Santo António 33
Santo António de Alfama 61
Santo Condestável 83
Santo Estevão 58, 59
Santos Oficios 67
São Cristovão 38
São Domingos 32
São Pedro de Alcântara 36
São Pedro Market 27
São Roque 33
São Tomé & Príncipe 39
São Vicente de Fora 32
Saramago, José 53
Sawasdee 103
Sé Catedral 6, **12–13**, 32, 57
Sebastião, Dom 30, 66
   tomb of 10, 11
security 108
self-catering accommodation 117
Senhor Vinho 43
Senhora da Guia 116
Senhora do Monte 36–7
Serra da Arrábida 52
Sertório Sauna Club 87
Setúbal 52
Seteais 101
Sheraton 115
shoes
   shoeshiners in Largo de São Domingos 66
   things to buy 41
   walking in Lisbon 111

shops
  Baixa to Restauradores 67
  bargaining in 110
  opening hours 110
  shopping districts 40–41
  things to buy 41
Silva, Aníbal Cavaco 31
Sintra 7, **26–7**, 52, 101
  drive to 101
  overcrowding at weekends 111
skateboarding 50–51
SNRIPD 108
Soares, Mário 31
Sofitel Lisbon Liberdade 112
Solar do Castelo 114
Solar do Embaixador 85
Solar dos Mouros 115
Solar do Vinho do Porto 73
Soul Club 39
souvenirs 41
Speakeasy 88
SS Bar 87
stainless steel cookware 41
stings, poisonous fish 108
Storytailors 74
sunbathing 108
Sundays, eating out 111
surfing 49
swimming
  safety 108
  swimming pools 51
Szenes, Arpad 35, 86

T
Tagus, river see Tejo
Tapada de Coelheiros wine 47
Tapas Bar 73
Tariq 31
Tasco do Chico 43
Tasquinha d'Adelaide 83, 89
Tavares 45, 77
taxis 106
Teatro Nacional Dona Maria II 66
Teatro Nacional de São Carlos 71
Tejo Estuary 37, 52
Tejo, river 18, 82, 106
telephones 109
television 109
Tenente, José António 74
Terra 89
theft 108

Tiara Park Atlantic Lisboa 112
tiles, Museu Nacional do Azulejo 7, **20–21**, 33, 34, 59
Timor 39
Timpanas 43
tipping 110
Tivoli Jardim 117
Tivoli Lisboa 112
Torralva, Diogo de 10, 21
Torre de Belém 7, **18–19**, 33, 84
Torre de São Lourenço 9
Torre de Ulisses 9
Torre Vasco da Gama 17
tourist office 107
tours, organized 106
traffic, safety 108
trains 106
trams 106
travel 106
Tróia 52
Tromba Rija 89
Trumps 87
Tryp Oriente 115

U
UK Embassy 107
Última Sé 60
Ulysses 30
UNESCO World Heritage sites, Sintra 7, **26–7**
Ursa 49, 53
US Embassy 107

V
vaccinations 108
Valentino Restauradores 69
Vallado wine 47
Varanda de Lisboa 69
Vasco da Gama bridge 82
Vasco, Grão (Vasco Fernandes) 35
Vasconcelos, Joana 34, 35
Vela Latina 18, 85
Verbasco 103
Vertigo 73, 75
Viagem de Sabores 61
Vieira da Silva, Maria Helena 35, 86
views 36–7
  hotels with 115
Vila Franca de Xira 53
Villalobos, Maria 12
Vincent, St 13, 32
VIP Eden 68

VIP Executive Suites Eden 117
Viriato 31
visas 107
Visigoths 30
Vista Alegre 74
Vitorino de Sousa 67

W
walks 49, 106
  Alfama, Castelo and the East 59
  Avenida & North Lisbon 93
  Baixa to Restauradores 65
  Chiado & Bairro Alto 73
  shoes for 111
  West Lisbon 83
water, drinking 108
Waterfront to Belém 86
weather 107
websites 107
West Lisbon (with Belém) 80–89
  gay Lisbon 87
  map 80
  nightlife 88
  restaurants 85, 89
  sights 84
  walks 83
Weyden, Rogier van der, St Catherine and St Joseph 25
when to go 107
Wi-Fi hotspots 109
Wine Bar do Castelo 60
wines 47
  Colares wine 100
  port 111
  Ribatejo Wine Route 53
  things to buy 41
women travellers 108

Y
York House 114

Z
Zé dos Bois (ZDB) 35
Zoo 50, 93

Acknowledgements

The Author

Tomas Tranæus is a travel writer, translator and photographer based in Lisbon and Madrid. He has contributed to *Eyewitness Portugal* and *Lisbon*, and to the *Time Out* guide to Lisbon. He also writes for Swedish publications.

The author would like to thank the editor for his cool grip and his courteous ways, and the main photographer for his amiable company.

Special thanks for his invaluable assistance to Carlos Oliveira, and to his colleagues at the Portuguese National Tourist Office, London, and the Lisbon Tourist Association, Lisbon.

Produced by Coppermill Books, 55 Salop Road London E17 7HS
Editorial Director Chris Barstow
Designer Ian Midson
Copy Editors Jane Oliver-Jedrzejak, Charles Phillips & Michael Wright
Proofreader Antony Mason
Indexer Hilary Bird
Main Photographer Antony Souter
Additional Photography Paul Bernhardt, Mark Harding, Linda Whitwam, Peter Wilson
Illustrator Chapel Design & Marketing
Maps Mapping Ideas

FOR DORLING KINDERSLEY
Publisher Douglas Amrine
Publishing Manager Fay Franklin
Design Managers Sunita Gahir, Mabel Chan
Senior Cartographic Editor Casper Morris
DTP Designer Natasha Lu
Production Controller Rita Sinha
Design and Editorial Assistance Emma Anacootee, Paul Bernhardt, Marta Bescos, Tessa Bindloss, Rhiannon Furbear, Mark Harding, Maite Lantaron, Rada Radojicic, Quadrum Solutions, Dora Whitaker

Picture Credits

Placement Key: t-top; tl-top left; tlc-top left centre; tc-top centre; tr-top right; cla-centre left above; ca-centre above; cra-centre right above; cl-centre left; c-centre; cr-centre right; clb-centre left below; cb-centre below; crb-centre right below; bl-bottom left, b-bottom; bc-bottom centre; bcl-bottom centre left; br-bottom right; d-detail. Every effort has been made to trace the copyright holders and we apologize in advance for any unintentional omissions. We would be pleased to insert the appropriate acknowledgements in any subsequent edition of this publication.

The publishers would like to thank the following individuals, companies and picture libraries for their kind permission to reproduce their photographs.

ALAMY IMAGES: imagebroker/ Florian Kopp 16-17c; James Nesterwitz 62tr; José Elias - Landmarks series 62cra BELÉM BAR CAFÉ - BBC: 42bl CORBIS: JAI/Camilla Watson 36tl IMAGES OF PORTUGAL: José Manuel 26tl; António Sacchetti 26bl; Bernardo Amaral 49tr; Joaquim Lobo 49br LEONARDO MEDIA LTD.: 112tr LUXFRAGIL: 42t MUSEU CALOUSTE GULBENKIAN, LISBON: 25tl MUSEU DA CIDADE, LISBON: 31tl NUTRICAFÉS SA: 68tc TOMAS TRANÆUS: 38tr, 38bl, 46tr, 51tr, 59cr, 60tl, 60tr, 61tl, 67tl, 67tr, 68tl, 68tr, 74tl, 74tr, 75tr, 76tr, 86tl, 87tl, 88tl, 88tr, 89tl, 94tr, 95tl, 107tl, 107tr, 109tl, 110tr, 111tl, 111tr, 112tl, 113tl, 114tl, 115tl, 116tr VELA LATINA: 85tl

All other images are © Dorling Kindersley. For further information see *www.dkimages.com*

Phrase Book

In an Emergency

Help!	**Socorro!**	soo-koh-roo
Stop!	**Páre!**	pahr'
Call a doctor!	**Chame um médico!**	shahm' ooñ meh-dee-koo
Call an ambulance!	**Chame uma ambulância!**	shahm' oo-muh añ-boo-lañ-see-uh
Call the police!	**Chame a polícia!**	shahm' uh poo-lee-see-uh
Call the fire brigade!	**Chame os bombeiros!**	shahm' oosh bom-bay-roosh

Communication Essentials

Yes	**Sim**	seeñ
No	**Não**	nowñ
Please	**Por favor/ Faz favor**	poor fuh-vor/ fash fuh-vor
Thank you	**Obrigado/da**	o-bree-gah-doo/duh
Excuse me	**Desculpe**	dish-koolp'
Hello	**Olá**	oh-lah
Goodbye	**Adeus**	a-deh-oosh
Yesterday	**Ontem**	oñ-tayñ
Today	**Hoje**	ohj'
Tomorrow	**Amanhã**	ah-mañ-yañ
Here	**Aqui**	uh-kee
There	**Ali**	uh-lee
What?	**O quê?**	oo keh
Which	**Qual?**	kwahl'
When?	**Quando?**	kwañ-doo
Why?	**Porquê?**	poor-keh
Where?	**Onde?**	oñd'

Useful Phrases

How are you?	**Como está?**	koh-moo shtah
Very well, thank you	**Bem, obrigado/da.**	bayñ o-bree-gah-doo/duh
Where is/are ...?	**Onde está/estão ...?**	oñd' shtah/shtowñ
How far is it to ...?	**A que distância fica ...?**	uh kee dish-tañ-see-uh fee-kuh
Which way to ...?	**Como se vai para ...?**	koh-moo seh vy puh-ruh
Do you speak English?	**Fala inglês?**	fah-luh eeñ-glehsh
I don't understand	**Não compreendo**	nowñ kom-pree-eñ-doo
Could you speak more slowly please?	**Pode falar mais devagar por favor?**	pohd' fuh-lar mysh d'-va-gar poor fuh-vor
I'm sorry	**Desculpe**	dish-koolp'

Useful Words

big	**grande**	grañd'
small	**pequeno**	pe-keh-noo
hot	**quente**	keñt'
cold	**frio**	free-oo
good	**bom**	boñ
bad	**mau**	mah-oo
open	**aberto**	a-behr-too
closed	**fechado**	fe-shah-doo
left	**esquerda**	shkehr-duh
right	**direita**	dee-ray-tuh
straight on	**em frente**	ayñ freñt'
near	**perto**	pehr-too
far	**longe**	loñj'
up	**para cima**	pur-ruh see-muh
down	**para baixo**	pur-ruh buy-shoo
early	**cedo**	seh-doo
late	**tarde**	tard'

entrance	**entrada**	eñ-trah-duh
exit	**saída**	sa-ee-duh
toilets	**casa de banho**	kah-zuh d' bañ-yoo
more	**mais**	mysh
less	**menos**	meh-noosh

Shopping

How much does this cost?	**Quanto custa isto?**	kwañ-too koosh-tuh eesh-too
I would like ...	**Queria ...**	kree-uh
I'm just looking	**Estou só a ver obrigado/a**	shtoh soh uh vehr o-bree-gah-doo/uh
Do you take credit cards?	**Aceita cartões de crédito?**	uh-say-tuh kar-toinsh de kreh-dee-too
What time do you open?	**A que horas abre?**	uh kee oh-rash ah-bre
What time do you close?	**A que horas fecha?**	uh kee oh-rash fay-shuh
This/that one	**Este/Esse**	ehst'/ehss'
expensive	**caro**	kah-roo
cheap	**barato**	buh-rah-too
size	**tamanho**	ta-man-yoo
white	**branco**	brañ-koo
black	**preto**	preh-too
red	**vermelho**	ver-mehl-yoo
yellow	**amarelo**	uh-muh-reh-loo
green	**verde**	vehrd'
blue	**azul**	uh-zool'
bakery	**padaria**	pah-duh-ree-uh
bank	**banco**	bañ-koo
bookshop	**livraria**	lee-vruh-ree-uh
cake shop	**pastelaria**	pash-te-luh-ree-uh
chemist	**farmácia**	far-mah-see-uh
market	**mercado**	mehr-kah-doo
newsagent	**kiosque**	kee-yohsk'
post office	**correios**	koo-ray-oosh

Sightseeing

cathedral	**sé**	seh
church	**igreja**	ee-gray-juh
garden	**jardim**	jar-deeñ
library	**biblioteca**	bee-blee-oo-teh-kuh
museum	**museu**	moo-zeh-oo
tourist information office	**posto de turismo**	posh-too d' too-reesh-moo
bus station	**estação de autocarros**	shta-sowñ d' oh-too-kah-roosh
railway station	**estação de comboios**	shta-sowñ d' koñ-boy-oosh

Staying in a Hotel

Do you have a vacant room?	**Tem um quarto livre?**	tayñ ooñ kwar-too leevr'
room with a bath	**um quarto com casa de banho**	ooñ kwar-too koñ kah-zuh d' bañ-yoo
shower	**duche**	doosh
single room	**quarto individual**	kwar-too een-dee-vee-doo-ahl'
double room	**quarto de casal**	kwar-too d' kuh-zahl'
twin room	**quarto com duas camas**	kwar-too koñ doo-ash kah-mash
I have a reservation	**Tenho um quarto reservado**	tayñ-yoo ooñ kwar-too-re-ser-vah-doo

Eating Out

Have you got a table for . . .?	**Tem uma mesa para . . . ?**	tayñ oo-muh meh-zuh puh-ruh
I want to reserve a table	**Quero reservar uma mesa**	keh-roo re-zehr-var o-muh meh-zuh
The bill please	**A conta por favor/ faz favor**	uh kohn-tuh poor fuh-vor/ fash fuh-vor
I am a vegetarian	**Sou vegetariano/a**	Soh ve-je-tuh-ree-ah-noo/uh
the menu	**a lista**	uh leesh-tuh
wine list	**a lista de vinhos**	uh leesh-tuh de veeñ-yoosh
glass	**um copo**	ooñ koh-poo
bottle	**uma garrafa**	oo-muh guh-rah-fuh
knife	**uma faca**	oo-muh fah-kuh
fork	**um garfo**	ooñ gar-foo
spoon	**uma colher**	oo-muh kool-yair
plate	**um prato**	ooñ prah-too
breakfast	**pequeno-almoço**	pe-keh-noo-ahl-moh-soo
lunch	**almoço**	ahl-moh-soo
dinner	**jantar**	jan-tar
starter	**entrada**	eñ-trah-duh
main course	**prato principal**	prah-too prin-see-pahl'
dessert	**sobremesa**	soh-bre-meh-zuh
rare	**mal passado**	mahl' puh-sah-doo
medium	**médio**	meh-dee-oo
well done	**bem passado**	bayñ puh-sah-doo

Menu Decoder

açorda	uh-sor-duh	bread-based stew
açúcar	uh-soo-kar	sugar
água mineral	ah-gwuh mee-ne-rahl'	mineral water
(com gás)	koñ gas	sparkling
(sem gás)	sayñ gas	still
alho	al-yoo	garlic
amêijoas	uh-may-joo-ash	clams
arroz	uh-rohsh	rice
atum	uh-tooñ	tuna
azeitonas	uh-zay-toh-nash	olives
bacalhau	buh-kuh-lyow	dried, salted cod
batatas	buh-tah-tash	potatoes
batatas fritas	buh-tah-tash free-tash	french fries
bica	bee-kuh	espresso
bife	beef	steak
bolo	boh-loo	cake
borrego	boo-reh-goo	lamb
café	kuh-feh	coffee
camarões	kuh-muh-roysh	large prawns
caranguejo	kuh-rañ-gay-joo	crab
carne	karn'	meat
cebola	se-boh-luh	onion
cerveja	sehr-vay-juh	beer
chouriço	shoh-ree-soo	red, spicy sausage
cogumelos	koo-goo-meh-loosh	mus
fiambre	fee-añbr'	ham
fígado	fee-guh-doo	liver
frango	frañ-goo	chicken
frito	free-too	fried
fruta	froo-tuh	fruit
gambas	gam-bash	prawns
gelado	je-lah-doo	ice cream
gelo	jeh-loo	ice
grelhado	grel-yah-d	squid
maçã	muh-sañ	apple
manteiga	mañ-tay-guh	butter
mariscos	muh-reesh-koosh	seafood
ostras	osh-trash	oysters

ovos	oh-voosh	eggs
pão	powñ	bread
pastel	pash-tehl'	cake
pato	pah-too	duck
peixe	paysh'	fish
pimenta	pee-meñ-tuh	pepper
polvo	pohl'-voo	octopus
porco	por-coo	pork
queijo	kay-joo	cheese
sal	sahl'	salt
salada	suh-lah-duh	salad
salsichas	sahl-see-shash	sausages
sopa	soh-puh	soup
sumo	soo-moo	juice
tamboril	tañ-boo-ril'	monkfish
tomate	too-maht'	tomato
vinho branco	veeñ-yoo brañ-koo	white wine
vinho tinto	veeñ-yoo teeñ-too	red wine
vitela	vee-teh-luh	veal

Numbers

0	**zero**	zeh-roo
1	**um**	ooñ
2	**dois**	doysh
3	**três**	tresh
4	**quatro**	kwa-troo
5	**cinco**	seeñ-koo
6	**seis**	saysh
7	**sete**	set'
8	**oito**	oy-too
9	**nove**	nov'
10	**dez**	desh
11	**onze**	oñz'
12	**doze**	doz'
13	**treze**	trez'
14	**catorze**	ka-torz'
15	**quinze**	keeñz'
16	**dezasseis**	de-zuh-saysh
17	**dezassete**	de-zuh-set'
18	**dezoito**	de-zoy-too
19	**dezanove**	de-zuh-nov'
20	**vinte**	veent'
21	**vinte e um**	veen-tee-ooñ
30	**trinta**	treeñ-tuh
40	**quarenta**	kwa-reñ-tuh
50	**cinquenta**	seen-kweñ-tuh
60	**sessenta**	se-señ-tuh
70	**setenta**	se-teñ-tuh
80	**oitenta**	oy-teñ-tuh
90	**noventa**	noo-veñ-tuh
100	**cem**	sayñ
101	**cento e um**	señ-too-ee-ooñ
200	**duzentos**	doo-zeñ-toosh
300	**trezentos**	tre-zeñ-toosh
400	**quatrocentos**	kwa-troo-señ-toosh
500	**quinhentos**	kee-nyeñ-toosh
700	**setecentos**	set'-señ-toosh
900	**novecentos**	nov'-señ-toosh
1,000	**mil**	meel'

Time

one minute	**um minuto**	ooñ mee-noo-too
one hour	**uma hora**	oo-muh oh-ruh
half an hour	**meia-hora**	may-uh-oh-ruh
Monday	**segunda-feira**	se-goon-duh-fay-ruh
Tuesday	**terça-feira**	ter-sa-fay-ruh
Wednesday	**quarta-feira**	kwar-ta-fay-ruh
Thursday	**quinta-feira**	keen-ta-fay-ruh
Friday	**sexta-feira**	say-shta-fay-ruh
Saturday	**sábado**	sah-ba-doo
Sunday	**domingo**	doo-meen-goo

Selected Street Index

Selected Street Index

1 de Dezembro, Rua	L3
24 de Julho, Avda	J6
5 de Outubro, Avda	F1
Academia das Ciências, Rua du	J3
Academia Nacional de Belas Artes, Largo da	L5
Adelino Amaro da Costa, Largo	N4
Afonso Costa, Avda	H1
Afonso Henriques, Alameda Dom	G1
Ajuda, Calçada da	B5
Alecrim, Rua do	K5
Alegria, Praça da	K1
Alexandre Herculano, Rua	F3
Alfândega, Rua da	N5
Almada, Rua do	J5
Almada, Travessa do	N4
Almirante Reis, Avda	G2
António Augusto de Aguiar, Avda	F2
António José de Almeida, Avda	G1
António Maria Cardoso, Rua	L5
António Pedro, Rua	G2
Arco da Graça, Rua do	M2
Arco Grande da Cima	Q3
Arsenal, Rua do	M5
Assunção, Rua da	M4
Ataíde, Rua do	K5
Augusta, Rua	M4
Augusto Rosa, Rua	N4
Áurea, Rua (Rua do Ouro)	M4
Bacalhoeiros, Rua dos	N5
Bartolomeu Dias, Rua	A6
Bélem, Rua de	B6
Beneficência, Rua da	F1
Benformoso, Rua do	N1
Berna, Avda de	F1
Bernardino Costa, Rua	L6
Betesga, Rua da	M3
Bica Duarte Belo, Rua da	K4
Boa Hora, Travessa da	K3
Boavista, Rua da	J5
Boqueirao de Ferreiros, Rua	J5
Braamcamp, Rua	F3
Cais de Santarém, Rua de	P5
Calouste Gulbenkian, Avda	E1
Caminhos de Ferro, Rua dos	R3
Capelo, Rua	L5
Carmo, Largo do	L4
Carmo, Rua do	L4
Carmo, Travessa do	L4
Cascais, Rua de	D5
Castelo, Costa do	N3
Cebolas, Campo das	N5
Ceuta, Avda de	D4
Chiado, Largo do	L4
Combatentes, Avda dos	E1
Combro, Calçada do	J4
Comércio, Praça do	M5
Comércio, Rua do	M5
Conceição da Glória, Rua da	K2
Conceição, Rua da	M5
Conde de Valbom, Avda	F1
Correeiros, Rua dos	M4
Correio Velho, Calçada do	N5
Crucifixo, Rua do	M4
Descobertas, Avda das	A5
Dom Carlos I, Avda	F4
Dom Luís I, Praça	J6
Dom Luís I, Rua de	J5

Dom Pedro V, Rua	K2
Dona Estefânia, Rua de	G2
Douradores, Rua dos	M4
Duarte, Rua dom	M3
Duque de Avila, Avda	F2
Duque de Terceira, Praça	K6
Durques de Bragança, Rua dos	L5
Eduardo Coelho, Rua	J3
Emensa, Rua de	K5
Engenheiro Duarte Pacheco, Avda	E3
Entrecampos, Rua da	F1
Escola Politécnica, Rua da	F3
Esperança, Rua da	F5
Estrela, Calçada da	E4
Estrela, Rua da	E4
Fanqueiros, Rua dos	M4
Ferreira Borges, Rua	E3
Figueira, Praça da	M3
Flores, Rua das	K5
Fontes Pereira de Melo, Avda	F2
Garrett, Rua	L4
Glória, Calçada dos	K3
Graça, Calçada da	P2
Graça, Largo da	P2
Guilherme Coussul, Travessa de	K5
Índia, Avda da	C6
Infante Santo, Avda	E4
Infate Dom Henrique, Avda	P5
Ivens, Rua	L4
Janelas Verdes, Rua das	E5
Jardim do Tabaco, Rua do	Q4
Jerónimos, Rua dos	B6
João das Regtras, Rua	M3
João V, Rua dom	E3
João XXI, Avda	G1
Joaquim António de Aguiar, Rua	F3
Jordão, Travessa do	N2
Junqueira, Rua da	C5
Lapa, Rua da	E4
Lavra, Calçada do	L1
Leite de Vasconcelos, Rua	Q1
Liberdade, Avda da	K1
Limoeiro, Rua do	P4
Loios, Largo dos	P4
Loreto, Rua do	K5
Luís de Camões, Praça	K4
Luisa Todi, Rua	K3
Madalena, Rua da	N4
Manuel da Maia, Avda	G1
Marcos do Penedo, Estrada	B4
Marquês de Fronteira, Rua	E2
Marquês de Pombal, Praça	F3
Martim Moniz, Praça	M2
Martim Moniz, Rua	N2
Miguel Bombarda, Avda	F1
Milagre de Santo António, Rua do	N4
Misericórdia, Rua da	L4
Monicas, Travessa das	P2
Monte, Calçada do	P1
Morais Soares, Rua	H2
Mouzinho de Albuquerque, Avda	H3
Município, Praça do	M5
Museu de Artilharia, Rua do	R3
Nova da Trindade, Rua	L4
Nova de São Domingos, Travessa	M3

Nova do Almanda, Rua	M5
Olarias, Rua das	N1
Paiva de Andrade, Rua	L5
Palma, Rua da	N1
Palmeira, Rua da	J2
Paraiso, Rua do	R2
Pedras Negras, Rua das	N4
Pedro Álvares Cabral, Avda	E3
Ponte, Avda da	D5
Portas de Santo Antão, Rua das	L2
Portas do Sol, Largo das	P4
Prata, Rua da	M4
Queluz, Estrada de	B4
Rato, Largo do	F3
Regueira, Rua da	P4
Remolares, Rua dos	K6
República, Avda da	F1
Restauradores, Praça dos	L2
Restelo, Avda do	A5
Ribeira das Naus, Avda da	L6
Ribeira Nova, Rua da	K5
Rodrigues de Freitas, Largo	P3
Rossio (Praça Dom Pedro IV)	M3
Salitre, Rua do	J1
Salvador, Rua do	P3
Santa Clara, Campo de	Q3
Santa Cruz do Castelo, Rua de	N3
Santa Justa, Rua de	M4
Santo Amaro, Calçada de	C5
Santo André, Calçada de	P2
Santo Estêvão, Rua de	Q4
São Bento, Rua	F4
São Bernardo, Rua de	F4
São Domingos, Largo de	M3
São Francisco, Calçada de	L5
São Julião, Rua de	M5
São Martinho, Largo	P4
São Miguel, Rua de	P4
São Nicolau, Rua de	M4
São Paulo, Rua de	K5
São Pedro de Alcântara, Rua de	K3
São Pedro, Rua de	P4
São Pedro, Travessa de	K3
São Tiago, Rua de	P4
São Tomé, Rua de	P3
São Vicente, Calçada de	Q3
São Vicente, Rua de	P3
Sapateiros, Rua dos	M4
Saraiva de Carvalho, Rua	E3
Saúde, Escada da	N2
Sé, Largo de	N5
Século, Rua do	J4
Senhora da Glória, Rua da	Q1
Senhora do Monte, Rua da	P1
Serpa Pinto, Rua	L5
Sidónio Pais, Avda	F2
Sodré, Cais de	K6
Tapada, Calçada da	D5
Telhal, Rua do	L1
Terreiro do Trigo, Rua do	Q4
Torre de Belém, Avda da	A6
Trindade Coelho, Largo	K3
Trindade, Rua da	L4
Vale de Santo António, Rua do	R1
Verónica, Rua da	Q2
Vitor Cordon, Rua	L5
Vitória, Rua da	M4
Voz do Operário, Rua da	P2